CHRIST'S NEW HOMELAND—AFRICA

Christ's New Homeland—Africa

Contribution to the Synod on the Family by African Pastors

Translated by
Michael J. Miller

IGNATIUS PRESS   SAN FRANCISCO

Cover art:
Detail of column capital depicting the Flight into Egypt
Cathedral St. Lazare, Autun, France
© Foto Marburg/Art Resource, New York

Cover design by Roxanne Mei Lum

© 2015 by Ignatius Press, San Francisco
All rights reserved
ISBN 978-1-62164-088-2
Library of Congress Control Number 2015948275
Printed in the United States of America ∞

CONTENTS

Berhaneyesus D. Cardinal Souraphiel, C.M., Metropolitan
Archbishop of Addis Abeba, President of the CBCE,
and Chairman of AMECEA

PART THREE

PASTORAL CARE OF FAMILIES THAT ARE HURTING

Christian Cardinal Tumi, Archbishop Emeritus of Douala,
Cameroon

Archbishop Antoine Ganye of Cotonou

Théodore Adrien Cardinal Sarr, Archbishop Emeritus of Dakar

Archbishop Samuel Kleda of Douala

EPILOGUE

AN APPEAL FROM THE CHURCH
IN AFRICA TO THE STATE

Jean-Pierre Cardinal Kutwa, Archbishop of Abidjan, Côte d'Ivoire

Preface

Francis Cardinal Arinze

The XIV General Assembly of the Synod of Bishops will sit in Vatican City from October 4 to 25, 2015, on the theme: "The Vocation and Mission of the Family in the Church and Contemporary World". It is fitting and beautiful that some distinguished African cardinals and bishops have put together their reflections on different aspects of this vital apostolate. The essays offered to the public in this present volume seem to me to be an excellent preparation for the forthcoming synod for the following reasons:

The African prelates make a concise presentation of the attitude of Africans toward marriage and the family. Africans see the family as a community of love between a man and a woman, with a loving opening to children. Marriage is the entry. It comes from the creating hands of God, and so no human being has the authority to try to reinvent it. A marriage in Africa establishes a link between the families of the man and the woman, with each side ready to help to make it a success. Appreciation of the complementarity of man and woman and of the divine origin of marriage and the family cuts across cultural, linguistic, and religious frontiers. To ignore the order established by the Creator in marriage and the family is to invite problems and sufferings on people and on society as a whole. The African prelates see the family in Africa as a place where the elders are highly respected, the link with the ancestors is appreciated, and the virtue of filial piety is extolled.

The authors of the articles in this book draw attention to the rich and beautiful teaching of the Magisterium of the Church on marriage and the family. Already *Gaudium et spes* (47) defines the family as "a community

Francis Cardinal Arinze is prefect emeritus of the Congregation for Divine Worship and the Discipline of the Sacraments.

of love". *Lumen gentium* (11) calls it "the domestic church", while *Apostolicam actuositatem* (11) sees it as "the first and vital cell of society". Blessed Paul VI in *Humanae vitae* presents Church teaching on responsible parenthood and defends conjugal morality. Pope Saint John Paul II in *Familiaris consortio*, *Letter to Families*, and *Evangelium vitae* goes into greater detail: "The future of humanity passes by way of the family", he says in *Familiaris consortio* 86. And in *Ecclesia in Africa* 43, he observes: "The African loves children, who are joyfully welcomed as gifts of God. 'The sons and daughters of Africa love life.'" Pope Benedict XVI, in *Africae munus* 43, insists that "The family needs to be protected and defended, so that it may offer society the service expected of it, that of providing men and women capable of building a social fabric of peace and harmony." Pope Francis at the solemn Mass in Manila on January 16, 2015, stoutly defended the family.

The Catechism of the Catholic Church teaches that "the home is the first school of Christian life and 'a school for human enrichment.' Here one learns endurance and the joy of work, fraternal love, generous—even repeated—forgiveness, and above all divine worship in prayer and the offering of one's life" (1657). Moreover, this *Catechism* allows no ambiguity on the purpose of marriage and the family: "Marriage and the family are ordered to the good of the spouses and to the procreation and education of children" (2201).

The reader of this book will notice that the prelates are not unaware of the forces that militate against marriage and the family in the world. Following the leadership of Pope Francis in Manila on January 16, 2015, they mention the new "ideological colonization" trends that seek to destroy the family and to introduce themselves also into the developing countries. The mass media are also used to banalize, secularize, and even commercialize marriage and the family. The prelates defend the unity and indissolubility of marriage and also the necessity of fidelity and openness to procreation.

In view of the fact that society in Africa, too, is made up of people of many religions, mixed marriages between a Catholic and a Christian of another denomination and interreligious marriages between a Christian and a person of another religious persuasion are current challenges on the African continent. Where the ideal of a Catholic man marrying a Catholic woman is not realized, the bishop and the parish priest have to assess the wisdom of permitting a mixed marriage or an interreligious one, after weighing the challenges involved. Under certain circumstances, such marriages may be able to promote ecumenism and interreligious collaboration, although this should not always be presumed.

The writings in this book see the task of the forthcoming synod of bishops as the promotion of good marriages. This calls for multiple actions on the part of Church personnel and, indeed, of all the faithful. There should be clear teaching on what the Church tells us about marriage and the family. Homilies, diocesan publications, and radio and television programs should bring sound Christian doctrine to the people. The writers have also stressed the importance of proper preparation for marriage, which should include not only catechetical instruction but also information on natural family planning. Engaged couples should be given adequate answers to contemporary errors regarding marriage and the family and sound teaching on chastity and its demands. The synod should insist that parishes and dioceses arrange courses for newly married couples to be given by well-chosen experienced couples. The importance of family prayers and frequent reception of the sacraments of penance and the Holy Eucharist also needs to be emphasized. The family as an active agent of evangelization, within itself and with other families, is also underlined by the writers.

Not all families are calm, happy, and peaceful. Some are wounded. The African prelates who have written this book did not forget such families. Some families have such wounds as divorce, single parenthood, childlessness, one spouse incurably sick or addicted to drugs, violence, infidelity, economic problems of a couple living together because of the pressures of work, war, or imprisonment, or sheer poverty and unemployment. Toward all such wounded families, the Church must, like Christ, be compassionate. It is Jesus who said: "Those who are well have no need of a physician, but those who are sick" (Mt 9:12). He is the "merciful and faithful high priest" (Heb 2:17). The prelates discuss how the Church can show mercy toward the divorced and remarried and toward people involved in polygamous marriages.

With regard to the divorced and remarried, the Church must take note that if a first marriage is valid, a second one cannot be approved. Pope Saint John Paul II has already, in *Familiaris consortio* 84, clearly stated that people involved in such second "marriages" cannot be admitted to Holy Communion because, otherwise, such action would be equivalent to declaring the first marriage dissolved, contrary to the clear teaching of Christ. The Church, however, does not abandon such members. She invites them to read and listen to the proclamation of the Word of God, to take part at Mass, to persevere in prayer, to engage in works of charity, to train their children in the Christian faith, and to engage in acts of penance. They can also approach Church tribunals to see if there are sound reasons for declaring the first marriage invalid from its very start.

In some parts of Africa, polygamy is practiced in some families. The prelates note that even in such countries, monogamy was practiced originally and is the norm in most families. The Church has the task of reinforcing the conviction that monogamy is the way forward. The practical problem is how to make credible and honorable arrangements for the other women so that the man can live with one wife and so that the Catholic community can be convinced of the sincerity and justice of the arrangements. The Plenary Assembly of the Symposium of Episcopal Conferences of Africa and Madagascar (SECAM) examined this challenge in 1978 and maintained the firm stand that polygamy cannot be approved.

The October 2015 Assembly of the Synod of Bishops has a vital pastoral matter on its agenda. African prelates have in this book rendered good service to the participants in this synod, to the Church in Africa, and to the Universal Church. I strongly recommend this work.

Vatican City
Solemnity of the Sacred Heart
June 12, 2015

Part One

The Synod on the Family:
From One Assembly to Another

What Sort of Pastoral Mercy in Response to the New Challenges to the Family?

A Reading of the *Lineamenta*

Robert Cardinal Sarah

The purpose assigned to the *Relatio synodi* that was sent by the Secretariat of the Synod of Bishops to the whole People of God, as the *Lineamenta*[1] for the next synod assembly, is "to raise questions and indicate points of view that will later be developed and clarified through reflection in the local Churches in the intervening year leading to the XIV Ordinary General Assembly of the Synod of Bishops" (*RS* 62).[2] The point of departure of this reflection is emphasized in the document clearly and in precise terms:

Robert Cardinal Sarah is prefect of the Congregation for Divine Worship and the Discipline of the Sacraments.

[1] The instruction given by the General Secretary of the Synod of Bishops, in his letter dated December 12, 2014, shows that the *Relatio synodi* was made the basis for discussion as the synod proceedings continued. "Accompanying this letter, which is being sent to episcopal conferences, the synods of the Eastern Catholic Churches *sui iuris*, the Union of Superiors General, and the Roman Curia, is a copy of the *Lineamenta* composed of the *Relatio synodi* and a series of questions on the reaction to this synodal document and a thorough examination of its contents, in the process of continuing the synodal journey already begun and in drafting the *Instrumentum laboris* for the next synodal assembly.

"The previously mentioned ecclesial entities are asked to choose a suitable manner to engage all components of the particular churches and academic institutions, organizations, lay movements, and other ecclesial associations in an ample consultation of the People of God on the family, within the framework of the synodal process."

[2] The paragraph numbering of the *Relatio synodi* given here follows that of the original document, which differs by one digit from that in the English translation provided by the Vatican website.—Trans.

Despite the many signs of crisis in the family institution in various areas of the "global village", the desire to marry and form a family remains vibrant, especially among young people, and serves as the basis of the need of the Church, an "expert in humanity" and faithful to her mission, to proclaim untiringly and with profound conviction the "Gospel of the Family", entrusted to her together with the revelation of God's love in Jesus Christ and ceaselessly taught by the Fathers, the masters of spirituality, and the Church's Magisterium. (RS 2)

On the basis of this clearly articulated teaching, the question that seems to dominate the *Relatio synodi* is how to address specific pastoral situations.

In the discussions both during the extraordinary assembly and after the synod, the constantly recurring concerns revolve around the pastoral path that is to be explored and its relation to the Church's doctrine about marriage and the family. The media coverage of this debate gives the impression that, on the one hand, there are those who are in favor of "closed doctrine" and, on the other hand, those who are for "pastoral openness". In reality, there is no doctrinal party opposed to a pastoral party; instead, both parties claim to be attached to the Church's perennial doctrine and want pastoral practice to express God's mercy toward everyone. Where, then, could there be a line of demarcation or even a breach? Would it be in the change of pastoral approach, since everyone seems to agree that the doctrine must be upheld? Might there be some, then, who would argue for the continuation of a pastoral practice that, if it changed, would *ipso facto* modify the doctrine?

1. From the development of doctrine to pastoral action

None of the bishops and cardinals in the Extraordinary Assembly of the Synod of Bishops who reacted vehemently to warn the entire Church about an obvious risk of a change of doctrine thought about doctrine as a fixed given. Although God's revelation of himself and of his loving plan for humanity was completed with Christ, its elaboration in the age of the Church by the Holy Spirit, the Paraclete, who leads us into all truth, is ongoing, along the lines indicated by Saint Vincent of Lerins in the *Commonitorium*. By affirming "quod ubique, quod semper, quod ab omnibus" (hold that faith which has been believed everywhere, always, by all), he points out a development in the doctrinal formulas, "yet only in its own kind; that is to say, in the same doctrine, in the same sense, and in the same meaning". This is a homogeneous development of dogma that the International Theological Commission would later reaffirm in its document on the interpretation of dogmas.[3] Therefore, even the "new scrutiny" called for in *Ad gentes* 22 will never mean an alteration of the revealed deposit of faith. Given the contemporary assumption that the Church must adopt her doctrine to what are called the "anthropological developments" in progress, we should recall that the norm of doctrine is not man but God himself. And however the times may change, God remains the same. "Tu autem idem Ipse es", the Psalmist exclaims (Ps 102:27): "O my God, ... you are [always] the same", whereas the face of the world changes incessantly.

It is true that "quod ubique" and "quod ab omnibus" are challenged more and more by a culture of "majority rule": the truth of the faith is no longer believed everywhere and by everyone within the Church, and some want to adjust it according to sociological trends. But the truth of the faith could never be subjected to such a standard. Peter Cardinal Erdö, President of the Council of the Bishops' Conferences of Europe (CCEE), recalled this recently while speaking to the participants in the CCEE-SECAM (Symposium of Episcopal Conferences of Africa and Madagascar) seminar on "The Joy of the Family" (Maputo, May 28–31, 2015): "We are not called to look at the world simply with our philosophical categories and only on the basis of empirical personal experiences or starting from sociological polls or studies, but we are disciples of Christ, so we must look to Christ, we must listen to his voice through history, through the Sacred Scripture, through the testimony of the community of the Church. ... Thus we see the direction: every real development in the Church draws us closer to Christ, both in faith and in daily life."

The media that amplify the issue of "the voice of the majority" forget to say that now most practicing Christians are found no longer in the Northern Hemisphere but rather in the Young Churches. Do they seek to listen to what the majority in these Young Churches have to say about issues that pertain to the future of the whole Church? Nothing could

[3] International Theological Commission, "On the Interpretation of Dogmas", *Origins* 20 (May 17, 1990): 1–14. This document was prepared under the direction of Professor Walter Kasper and published in 1990 with the authorization of Joseph Cardinal Ratzinger, president of the commission.

be farther from the truth. They scarcely let them speak, if they are not actually trying to confine them to issues that are depicted as "taboos"!

As for the development of pastoral practice, those who decry the Church's rigidity in matters of sexual morality think that the God who revealed himself in time as the God of love and tenderness used a pedagogy to which the Church no longer seems to pay attention. New developments in pastoral practice would not mean changing doctrine, they maintain, but rather would allow the Church to make God's loving heart more apparent and accessible. But could they seriously think that the bishops and cardinals who were warning about a real danger of doctrinal deviation have a fixed concept of pastoral practice? If God's pedagogy changes, that of the Church should not become rigid. And since in his pedagogy God gives himself, this pedagogy should not and could not change the content of the truth that is to be proposed to human freedom. The same goes for the pastoral practice of the Church: although it has often changed, depending on the times and the places, this could only be in the sense in which John Paul II described the new evangelization: "new in its ardor, new in its methods, and new in its expressions".[4] Therefore, faced with new challenges, the Church knows that she must change her pastoral practice; but she cannot do so by denying herself, for her *modus essendi*, her way of being, is the way of being of Jesus Christ, the Good Shepherd, who is the same yesterday, today, and for all eternity (Heb 13:8).

On the basis of this preliminary twofold clarification, it is appropriate now to evaluate the *Relatio synodi (RS)*—since the *Lineamenta* has reopened the discussion of it—and to see how we might arrive at a deeper appreciation of it.

2. *The* Relatio synodi

The document is made up of sixty-two paragraphs grouped by topic into three parts: "listening", then "looking", and finally "discussion"—a discussion extended by the questionnaire added by the Secretariat of the Synod of Bishops so as to allow the local Churches to continue the reflection begun at the Extraordinary General Assembly of the Synod of Bishops.

[4] An expression used for the first time by Pope John Paul II during his pilgrimage to Poland in 1979; he repeated it on March 9, 1983, in his address to the Episcopal Council of Latin America (CELAM) in Port-au-Prince, Haiti.

The *RS* reported first on how the Synod Fathers listened to the reality of the family today, in all its complexity, with its bright spots and shadows. The social and cultural context in which this familial reality is apprehended is that of a rapid "anthropological and cultural change" that influences all aspects of life in society.[5] One of the major forms of poverty in contemporary culture, the document says, is loneliness, "arising from the absence of God in a person's life and the fragility of relationships" (*RS* 6). Within this context, one focus of attention is emotional life, an affectivity that the modern world would like to be limitless, an affectivity, according to the surrounding culture, "in which every aspect needs to be explored, even those which are highly complex" (*RS* 10). The pastoral challenge that then presents itself to the Church is "the need to offer a word of truth and hope" in such a way that it finds the listener "responsive to humanity's most profound expectations" (*RS* 11).

In order to take up this challenge, the document proposes a look at Jesus and the divine pedagogy in the history of salvation. It recalls that the look of Jesus himself was full of love and tenderness toward the women and men whom he encountered, "accompanying their steps with truth, patience, and mercy, in proclaiming the demands of the Kingdom of God" (*RS* 12). As for God's pedagogy in salvation history, it consisted of three fundamental stages that reveal God's plan for marriage and the family: the original family, Moses' concession for a union damaged by sin, and marriage and the family as redeemed by Christ and restored to the image of the Most Holy Trinity. The document then goes on to present this mystery over the centuries in the teaching of the Church, especially after Vatican II (*RS* 17–20). The indissolubility of marriage and the joy of living together are emphasized (*RS* 21–22) as well as the truth and beauty of the family (*RS* 23). The document congratulates couples who remain faithful to this teaching and encourages those whose love has been wounded and yet continue to live in faithfulness (ibid.). Finally, it turns to those who live in situations contrary to the evangelical truth of marriage and the family (*RS* 24–28). Concern for this last-mentioned category dominates part 3, the discussion of pastoral perspectives.

---

[5] This anthropological change is manifested in a more radical, more secularized way in the West. The nihilist ideology of the new cultural revolution aims at establishing a new society and a new concept of man. Man must be recreated, and society must be remade without God.

It is a matter of proclaiming the Gospel of the Family today in various settings, while recalling that the truth of Jesus "became flesh in human weakness, not to condemn it but to save it" (RS 29). The document insists that the Church should adapt her language and be content, not "in merely presenting a set of rules, but in espousing values" (RS 33). It also calls for "a thorough renewal of the Church's pastoral practice" (RS 37). Many Synod Fathers insisted on a "renewal in the training of priests, deacons, catechists, and other pastoral workers" in this area (ibid.), so that they might be more careful in guiding future spouses who are preparing for marriage and in accompanying their first years of married life; they should also be able to provide appropriate pastoral care to those faithful who are in a civil marriage or are cohabiting and to care for wounded families (separated couples, persons who are divorced but not remarried, divorced and remarried persons, one-parent families). They will also be expected to provide pastoral care for persons who have a homosexual orientation.

Finally, the document devotes several paragraphs to the question of the transmission of life and the challenge of underpopulation (RS 57–59), the challenge of education, and the role of the family in evangelization (RS 60–61). The conclusion notes that the questions raised by the document should be developed and clarified before the next synod assembly.

The merit of the document is that it captured the spirit in which the discussions were conducted at the synod and the great freedom with which each Synod Father was able to speak about any questions and to propose perspectives that seemed to him pastorally appropriate in conducting the Church's mission to families today. But in this report there is also some confusion and even some serious errors that need to be pointed out, because, coming from an official Roman body, they could very well be troubling and confusing for those whose consciences are weak.

• A perplexing point

In paragraph 14, the document seems to insinuate that insisting on the indissolubility of marriage would be synonymous with subjugating persons, and it gives the impression that it takes the Mosaic model for granted, since, it says, Jesus himself refers to it. Are we supposed to return, then, to the era of "hardness of heart" in the pre-Gospel period? Yet on closer inspection of the Gospel passage, it appears also that the way in which Jesus speaks about marriage under the Mosaic law is instead a condemnation of this "hardness of heart", which is obviously unfaithful to the original truth. John Paul II taught this already in his *Theology of the Body*:

> On the basis of the above analyses of Christ's appeal to the "beginning" in his discourse on the dissolubility of marriage and the "certificate of divorce," it is evident that he clearly sees the fundamental contradiction contained in the marriage law of the Old Testament inasmuch as it accepted effective polygamy, that is, the institution of concubines in addition to legitimate wives, or the right of cohabitation with a slave woman. One can say that this law, while *combating sin, at the same time* contained in itself *the "social structures of sin"*; in fact, it *protected* and legalized them. In these circumstances, the essential ethical meaning of the commandment "Do not commit adultery" necessarily suffered a fundamental revaluation.[6]

With this clarification, it is difficult to consider the era of hardheartedness as a transitional stage that would gradually lead toward evangelical perfection. That said, Christ, in his teaching about marriage, makes this transition with an authority that puts him in a different league from that of the scribes, as the crowds said. The Church, following both Saint John and Saint Paul, has always professed and taught throughout her history that his very person is the Grace given by the Father to elevate natural marriage—and not legalized adultery—to its perfection as a sacrament.[7]

When we come to the episode of the Samaritan woman, mentioned by the *Relatio synodi*, we see clearly that Jesus, when he met her, brought her to make a confession and led her to a change of life, as we can reasonably deduce from the continuation of the episode. In the life of the aforementioned adulterous woman, was there not a "before" and an "after"? Would the "new pastoral approach" of which the document speaks not consist, therefore, of having our brothers and sisters who are

---

[6]John Paul II, *Man and Woman He Created Them: A Theology of the Body*, trans. Michael Waldstein (Boston: Pauline Books & Media, 2006), catechesis 36.1, p. 271.

[7]On this argument, see Aline Lizotte, "Réflexions sur le Synode extraordinaire", *AFCP* (October 2014): 5–6. See also Gerhard Cardinal Müller, *On the Indissolubility of Marriage and the Debate concerning the Civilly Remarried and the Sacraments* (2013), published by the Congregation for the Doctrine of the Faith.

in situations objectively contrary to the truth of the Gospel encounter Jesus Christ, so that in spirit and in truth this encounter might result in a call to begin a new life? The Gospel tells us that the company of Jesus was made up of converted sinners, does it not?

• Unacceptable, scandalous points

From the perplexing, we move on to the unacceptable. Could it be that the document is advocating trial marriage as a path to be followed? Paragraph 27 reads:

> In this regard, a new aspect of family ministry is requiring attention today—the reality of civil marriages between a man and woman, traditional marriages, and, taking into consideration the differences involved, even cohabitation. When a union reaches a particular stability, legally recognized, characterized by deep affection and responsibility for children and showing an ability to overcome trials, these unions can offer occasions for guidance with an eye towards the eventual celebration of the sacrament of marriage. Very often, on the other hand, a couple lives together not in view of a possible future marriage but without any intention of a legally binding relationship.

To what population does the document address this reality of civil marriages as a preparation for sacramental marriage? To the baptized members of the Church or to sympathetic pagans in areas where an initial evangelization is being conducted? Unless it applies to the neo-pagans in the countries of former Christendom!

At a time when, in the Young Churches, pastors persistently exhort young people who, very often, put off sacramental marriage for reasons unrelated to lukewarmness in the faith or relativism (that is, because of social pressures connected with their fertility and their economic status), it is disconcerting to read in the *Lineamenta*, after having heard it in the extraordinary assembly, that a period of "civil" marriage may be recommended as a phase in which a couple's relationship can mature. In many regions of Africa where customs prescribe an "indissoluble traditional marriage"—one that is therefore more stable than civil marriage—the local Church is not even authorized to use such language. If she did, not only would she ruin her pastoral ministry to families, but she would also be in contradiction with the Gospel and would scandalize the pagans.

- The results of confusion: Set God and doctrine aside, and you create major pastoral confusion

Unfortunately we find slippery language in the document, with treacherous expressions in the midst of doctrinally correct statements. We observe also that dissimilar situations are linked misleadingly. Are situations that "do not yet" correspond to the Gospel message of the same nature as those that "no longer correspond" to that ideal (RS 41)?

To get out of the amalgamation that we see in paragraph 42, which cites a jumble of motives for *de facto* cohabitation that are by no means based on the same reasons, would it not be more appropriate to make clear distinctions? Should situations directly connected with the decline of faith be confused with those in which other factors play a part?

It is astonishing that the same document that clearly notes in paragraph 5 that there is a "crisis of faith, witnessed among a great many Catholics, which oftentimes underlies the crisis in marriage and the family" draws no conclusions from that fact. Why does it not say that the first challenge to address is the crisis of faith? Why does it seek, in one particularly disconcerting perspective, to proceed to renew the Church's way of speaking about situations that are objectively contrary to the Gospel as though it were merely a matter of "words" or "language" (cf. RS 33)? This document is correct when it says that "one symptom of the great poverty of contemporary culture is loneliness, arising from the absence of God in a person's life and the fragility of relationships" (RS 6), is it not? Why does it not emphasize that the only solution is to make God present once again in people's lives? Unless it is because some trends are crying out for Communion for those who no longer live in the truth of the Gospel of the Family!

When we are talking about communion with God, there really is no third way. We explained this in our recent book *God or Nothing*. Either we choose the way that leads us to God—and it is the narrow way of which Christ speaks—or else we take the broad way of the world that leads us away from God. When Yahweh sets before his people the way of good and the way of evil and asks them to choose, he exhorts them to choose the way of good so that they might live. For this reason, we sought, throughout this book, for the benefit of our contemporaries, to place God back at the center of our thoughts, at the center of our action, and at the center of our lives, and at the place that he alone must occupy, so that our journey as Christians might be centered on this Rock and this firm assurance of our faith.

Indeed, the lack of a clear position and all the confusion that we note in the *Relatio synodi* are obvious signs, not only of a deep crisis of faith, but also of an equally deep crisis in pastoral practice: pastors hesitate to set out clearly in one direction. In seeking to respond to the latter crisis, certain pastoral attitudes described as "new" are rather haphazardly recommended. Now the Church, deeply rooted in doctrine, has a great pastoral tradition in which she has always accompanied "with attention and care the weakest of her children". In places where the Church is truly on her mission, has she failed to be "a beacon", "a torch" "for those who have lost their way" (cf. *RS* 28)? Yet does the "beacon of a lighthouse in a port" not guide safely because it is fixed?

The Church's pastoral ministry, as her pastors strive to conduct it in the Young Churches, has never outlawed from the community those who are in difficult marital situations. On the contrary, in most cases, they are active members in ecclesial life. The fact that they do not go to sacramental Communion—which is not in their view a simple communal meal from which they would feel excluded—nevertheless does not diminish their profound desire to serve Jesus and his ecclesial community. Of course they do suffer because of their situation—because they want to receive the Body of Christ in truth—but they do not despair. The whole Christian community, indeed, helps them, by its prayers and by its way of behaving toward them, to hold fast to the hope of returning to the sacraments before their death, when the objective impediment will be removed from their lives. They are at home in the ecclesial communities: base communities and parish communities and, within them, prayer groups, regular devotions, charitable associations, Catholic Action, charismatic movements, et cetera.

This pastoral life is lively and warm because it is supported by the simple, trusting faith of Christ's faithful. They are aware that life is not a round of pleasure; yet in the midst of tragedies and spiritual combat, they feel supported by Holy Mother Church, whom they do not judge, as we see unfortunately today in many of the countries that formerly brought us this treasure of the faith.

The question that the document ought to have emphasized as the main problem to be faced by the Church, especially in the countries of former Christendom, is how to revive the faith within families. This is the prerequisite for a true renewal of pastoral care of the family within our communities, pastoral practice that will guide each family and, within it, each Christian to encounter God personally and to experience intimately his unfathomable love for each of us.

In this area of the renewal of pastoral care to the family, the Holy Spirit preceded us by creating in his Church, more than thirty years ago, a prophetic initiative on behalf of the family: the Pontifical John Paul II Institute for Studies on Marriage and Family and all the related pastoral works carried out by the Pontifical Council for the Family. Africa very soon grasped the importance of the initiative of the saintly Pope Wojtyła, and throughout the continent, episcopal commissions for the family, diocesan commissions for the family, and groups and movements for the family are at work.

It is astonishing, therefore, that instead of a more in-depth study and an organized, systematic diffusion of this great pastoral effort deployed by John Paul II, some speak as though nothing had been done to be close to families, and they narrow the perspective to an opposition between those who are allegedly fixated on legalism and those who invoke the Divine Mercy. The reader is likewise surprised by the total silence in the *Lineamenta* about the Theology of the Body, which develops the authentic theology of marriage and family. Instead, there is a single-minded focus on a theology of love with no connection to the mystery of the nuptial fulfillment that God instituted by creating man in his likeness, by creating them male and female (cf. Gen 1:27).

In fact, one guesses that the *Relatio synodi* is actually the reflection of a malaise of the Church in the West—a Church stifled by a secularized, godless society—but also because of her particular history, in which she feels as though imprisoned in a pastoral approach that seems to offer more rules than values (*RS* 33). The Western Church therefore feels the need to change this perspective, the need for a pastoral approach that pays more attention to the weak and wounded members, to the school of the Good Shepherd. But is it not strange, sad, and even dangerous to pit divine laws and canonical norms in this way against values, when these norms are the synthetic, comprehensive expression of doctrine in the service of life—precisely what we call pastoral ministry?

It would not be fair, however, to generalize about the particular deficiencies observed here and there in the West. There are many doctrinally well-grounded pastors who are completely devoted to the suffering members of their communities. And they understand very well the danger in taking shortcuts while trying to settle sacramentally a question that is on the order of pastoral care.

A certain pastoral emphasis that is insufficiently enlightened theologically, in which the sacraments appear to be the "sole" mediation of grace, has created much confusion and serious damage within the Christian people. However, as the Catholic Church sees it, our separated brethren (in this case, Protestants who do not have the sacrament of the Eucharist) are not depicted as "condemned to hell" or even considered as "excluded from communion with Christ". Well, then, why would anyone accuse the Church of doing that with regard to her own children who have not denied a single article of the Church's Creed? Can we really uphold the Catholic doctrinal approach in the ecumenical dialogue and at the same time muddy our language about the place assigned to our brethren in difficulty within the Catholic Church?

If we admit to Holy Communion the lay faithful who have divorced and then civilly remarried, why would we reject the lay faithful who had become polygamous? We would even also have to remove "adultery" from the list of sins (can. 1856)!

Some ask the Church to change her language, but if a change of language is in order, it seems clear to us that it should be made by those who practice the art of confusing matters by shifting problems away from where they really arise. "Communion alone is not the solution: the solution is integration", Pope Francis reminded us. Therefore, it is a question of how pastors and the whole community behave toward these brethren so that they do not feel rejected, even though their situation is of their own making.

• A final surprise

It is astonishing that the document assigns so little importance to the very serious problem of declining birthrates and to the family's role in evangelization. Similarly, the offhand remark about education—as though to say, at the end of the document, that they have not forgotten this aspect—is surprising. Now the crisis of faith and the crisis of pastoral ministry are accompanied in reality by the crisis of education. We must resume our task of educating in the light of the Gospel and make a serious investment in this ministry, so as not to have to seek after the fact to fill in a breach between faith and culture that has already become an abyss.

Another dangerous ambivalence in the document: "Parents, then, [should be] able freely to choose the type of education for their children, according to their convictions" (*RS* 60). In a secularized and highly individualized society in which references to values are subjective and relativistic, the norm of Christian education cannot be reduced to "our convictions" but must be presented clearly as the person of Jesus Christ and the Gospel values he proclaims. For the Church has no other norm than Jesus Christ himself.

The document seems to attribute to the speech of pastors power to revive the fruitfulness of the contemporary anthropology, and therefore it resorts to the very fundamental notion of mercy. But everyone agrees that the anthropology that is widespread today, especially in the West, is quite the opposite of the anthropology of man created in the image and likeness of God. It seems very strange to call this postmodern anthropology fruitful, and even stranger the speech of a pastor who would be content to play on words so as to revive what is called fruitfulness.

After these brief notes about what seem to us to be serious limitations of the *Relatio synodi*, which are preserved unchanged in the *Lineamenta* and which we hope to find corrected by the *Instrumentum laboris*, we must address the pastoral concern that runs through the document: What path should be taken for pastoral mercy?

3. What sort of pastoral mercy?

The *Lineamenta* indicate that in the much larger ecclesial context described by *Evangelii gaudium*, the new path marked out by the extraordinary synod takes as its point of departure "life's periphery", which calls for a pastoral approach characterized by the "culture of encounter ... capable of recognizing the Lord's gratuitous work, even outside customary models, and of confidently adopting the idea of a 'field hospital', which is very beneficial in proclaiming God's mercy" (introduction to the questions on the *Relatio synodi*, part I).

The question to be asked, then, is: What are these peripheries of life in the new socio-cultural context that we face today?

The impact of globalization on human cultures has been so destructive that not only traditional social institutions but also the values that sustain them have been shaken to their foundations. Through political and legislative power (for example, new laws deconstructing the family and marriage and speculating on human life), financial power (developmental aid contingent on the adoption of "anti-family" and "anti-life" documents), and especially the power of the media, a relativistic ideology is being spread through all our contemporary societies. If we are to believe the president of the CCEE, in the countries of the Northern Hemisphere "*de facto* cohabitation has now become the norm",[8] which sociological studies confirm. Living in a Christian family, according to Gospel values, has become a marginal situation in relation to the majority. Christian families, in this context, are now not just numerically in the minority, but they are also in a sociological minority. They are experiencing silent but oppressive and relentless discrimination: everything is against them, the prevailing values, media and cultural pressure, financial constraints, legislation, and so on. And the Church herself, through documents like the *Lineamenta*, seems to be pushing them toward the exit.

If the *Lineamenta* are expressed in the language we have just seen, what sort of Church, then, will take care of this "little remnant"? Who will make it hear the merciful voice of the Good Shepherd, saying to it repeatedly: "Fear not, little flock" (Lk 12:32)?

Have we not reached here the real "periphery" of our postmodern global village? We will hope that the next synod will not chase from the "Cave of Bethlehem" (the Church) the little Christian family that has found no room in the inns of the "City of King David" (our globalized world). The beautiful Christian families that are heroically living out the demanding values of the Gospel are today the real peripheries of our world and of our societies, which are going through life as though God did not exist.

Besides this "little remnant", there is a second category that is loudly crying out for pastoral attention. These are the victims of the postmodern system who do not admit defeat. They do not feel at home in this godless world. They bear within them nostalgia for the warmth of the "Christian home", but they do not feel they have the strength to return to that radically evangelical way of life. To these people, we seem to

[8] Message from the President of CCEE, Peter Cardinal Erdö, Archbishop of Esztergom-Budapest, to the CCEE-SECAM Seminar, "The Joy of the Family", Maputo, May 28–31, 2015.

present today a rigid Church, a Mother who no longer understands them and shuts the door in their face. And some try to convince them that they are judged and condemned by the very people who ought to welcome them and care for them. Instead of helping them to discover the horror of sin and to beg to be delivered from it, no one has the right to hold out to them a sort of "mercy" that accomplishes nothing but lets them sink deeper into evil.

But these brothers and sisters who have truly been wounded by life are not fooled by it. They thirst for the truth about their life, not for pity or mollifying talk. They know very well that they are victims of the globalized system that aims to weaken and destroy the Church. They are not among those who give voice to relativistic ideologies so as to undermine the foundations of Christian doctrine and to nullify the Cross of Christ.

They see themselves as the sinner of whom Saint Augustine speaks, who, although he does not resemble God by the sinlessness that he has lost, wishes at least to resemble him by his horror of sin.[9] This, indeed, is why they do not want anyone to prevent them from crying out to heaven: "Who will show us salvation?", "Jesus, son of David, have pity on me!", by promising them something that Christ never promised to give.

God has never shut his heart against these brothers and sisters, and the Church, his Servant, cannot do so, either. But how can the Church take up a pastoral approach of mercy toward them? By not bandaging with sacramental Communion a wound that has not been treated by the sacrament of reconciliation duly received.

If her pastoral approach must not be denunciation, which mistreats the injured person who already has a bleeding wound, but rather compassionate presence, then the Church cannot pretend to be unaware of the real existence of the ravages caused by the wound; instead, she must apply the balm of her heart, so that this wound might be treated and bandaged with a view to true healing. This sort of respectful presence, with the renewed way of seeing things that comes from God, will

---

[9] "We should be displeased with ourselves when we commit sin, for sin is displeasing to God. Sinful though we are, let us at least be like God in this, that we are displeased at what displeases him. In some measure then you will be in harmony with God's will, because you find displeasing in yourself what is abhorrent to your Creator" (Saint Augustine, *Sermon on the Old Testament*, 19, 2–3; CCL 41, 252–54).

therefore never call "good" something that is evil or something that is good, "evil", as the ritual for the Ordination of Bishops reminds them. It is a pastoral approach of hope and expectation, as the merciful Father waits for his prodigal son. Like the Good Shepherd, the Church will have to go and seek her children who are far away, take them on her shoulders, hold them tight, and not put them back into the brambles that have torn up their lives. This is the meaning of pastoral mercy.

It is the mercy of the Father waiting for his prodigal child, who decides to abandon his life of misery among the pigs and to walk, transformed interiorly, to his Father's house so that the latter might give him the heart of a son, clothe him in a wedding garment, and place on his finger the ring of the New Covenant (Lk 15).

The brothers and sisters who are touched in this way by the tender, merciful heart of God will be able to find in the "little remnant" of Christian families a "friendly home" that welcomes them, that lives with them in the Church; through this contact, the flame of the "desire to start a family" can be reborn in their lives.

Together, all together, these brothers and sisters will be able to go out on a mission into the secularized world that believes in neither God nor the devil nor in humanity and is ruining its own anthropological foundations. As authentic apostles of the Lord, they will be able to testify to what God's mercy is doing authentically in their lives. They will show by their very style of involvement that the much-discussed new pastoral approach can develop only within the larger dynamic of the new evangelization: "new in its ardor, new in its methods, and new in its expressions".

Within such a missionary perspective, pastors are invited to listen again to Yahweh's warnings to the shepherds of Israel and to meditate again on the brilliant commentary on it that Saint Augustine wrote:[10] "The weak you have not strengthened, the sick you have not healed, the crippled you have not bound up, the strayed you have not brought back, the lost you have not sought, and with force and harshness you have ruled them. So they [my sheep] were scattered, because there was no shepherd; and they became food for all the wild beasts" (Ezek 34:4–5). While trying to deal with the weak and wounded sheep, one must not overwhelm those who are strong. The Lord certainly said, with respect

---

[10] Saint Augustine, *Sermon on Pastors*, CCL 41.

to the shepherd who lost one sheep, that he left the ninety-nine others who had not strayed to go look for the one who was lost. Is this why the *Relatio synodi* decided to pass a little too quickly over the families that are striving—some of them heroically—to be faithful to the Gospel, only to dwell on the case of wounded families? But the Lord did not say that we should blame the sheep who have not gone astray, as though they were the reason why the lost sheep strayed. Nor did he ask us to burden them; on the contrary, he rebukes the shepherds for the mistreatment they have inflicted on the strong sheep: "Should not the shepherds feed the sheep? You ... slaughter the fatlings" (Ezek 34:2–3). How did they slaughter them? By giving them bad example,[11] Saint Augustine says; by scandalizing them, we might add, by this pressure that tries to oblige them to recognize positive values in situations that are contrary to the Gospel. Saint Augustine says that for these pastors, their sheep are dead, and if they are still alive, it is thanks to Jesus Christ: "Do what they say, but not what they do"; for they say what they say in the name of Jesus, but what they do they do in their own name. But if what they say is contrary to what the Lord says, what a tragedy!

No Christian who loves the Church can remain unmoved by the fact that the extraordinary synod, in allowing the text of the *Relatio post disceptationem* to be published, in spite of itself became the accomplice of certain groups that, with the help of the media, seriously offended God by peddling his word (2 Cor 2:17) and placed a heavy burden on families that are heroically following Jesus in the midst of a world that is determined to destroy the family.

Let us listen again to Saint Augustine: "What sort of shepherds are they who for fear of giving offense not only fail to prepare the sheep for the temptations that threaten, but even promise them worldly happiness? God himself made no such promise to this world."[12] And citing the example of the apostle Saint Paul, he says that he did not hesitate "to cut the wound and not to spare the diseased part",[13] precisely out of mercy toward the injured sheep.

Therefore it is not possible to find "human values" or "positive values" in forms of union that are objectively contrary to the Gospel, as the *Relatio synodi* asserts (*RS* 41). Although Catholic doctrine

[11] Cf. Saint Augustine, Sermon 46, 9.
[12] Saint Augustine, Sermon 46, 10–11.
[13] Saint Augustine, Sermon 46, 6–7.

has never reduced the sinner to his sin—because the Lord never did so—it nevertheless declares it to be contrary to revelation to think that one could find some "good" in sinful relations. Making someone who is in this situation understand that he, too, is loved by God is not the same as telling him that his situation involves aspects that in no way sadden the God of mercies. If that were the case, the Son of God would not have died on the Cross for sinners. No one disputes the fact that there is some good in the lives of those who find themselves in situations not in keeping with the Gospel, but it is unacceptable to seek good in their form of life. For all those acts that, in the Church's moral tradition, are called intrinsically evil (*intrinsice malum*) are evil always and in themselves, in other words, because of their very object, independently of the circumstances and the ulterior motives of the person who acts. Hence, without in any way denying the influence that circumstances and especially intentions have on morality, the Catholic Church teaches that "there are acts which, in and of themselves, independently of circumstances and intentions, are always gravely illicit by reason of their object."[14]

Pastoral care of persons who are living in a civil union or cohabiting (*RS* 41–43) must be based on nothing other than a clear, firm proposal of Christian marriage and its requirements. It must not be based on any other "good" but the one provided in Christian marriage. Let each one therefore take care how he tries to build the Church of the Lord (cf. 1 Cor 3:10)!

But why would the Church be afraid or ashamed to live in a way different from the ways of the world? Why would the Church give up being the light of truth for the people? Why would she not accept her status as a "little flock" at the heart of a godless world? What does she fear? She is in the world but not of it, and is she not sent to this world by the One who assures her of his presence until the end of time? What would she have to contribute to this world if the things of this world ever became her norm? If those who brought the faith to Africa

---

[14] "It is therefore an error to judge the morality of human acts by considering only the intention that inspires them or the circumstances (environment, social pressure, duress or emergency, etc.) which supply their context. There are acts which, in and of themselves, independently of circumstances and intentions, are always gravely illicit by reason of their object; such as blasphemy and perjury, murder and adultery. One may not do evil so that good may result from it" (*Catechism of the Catholic Church* 1756).

no longer have the courage to ask these questions, we recently grafted branches are so bold as to make these inquiries, for the good of all, we believe.

Conclusion: Nova Patria Christi—Africa

As the starting date for the XIV General Ordinary Assembly of the Synod of Bishops dedicated to "The Vocation and Mission of the Family in the Church and Contemporary World" approaches, the particular Churches, the theological faculties, and groups and associations of families are intensifying their preparations for this major ecclesial event. At the same time, there is a sense that opinion makers, pressure groups, and lobbies are coming to the fore. We also see communications strategies being implemented; it would even seem that new methodologies for the synod assembly are being examined in order to give a voice to some lines of thought while endeavoring to make others inaudible, if not to silence them completely. Everything leads us to believe that the next synod assembly will be for many people a synod with high stakes. The future of the family is indeed at stake for mankind today. This is even more true for the Church, of which it is "the first and the most important path" (John Paul II).[15]

Faced with such a high-stakes event, Christian Africa wishes to make its modest contribution. But she wants to do so with clarity and determination, aware that it is part of the mission that the first three postconciliar popes prophetically left to her and for which Pope Francis unceasingly encourages her by constantly exhorting her to resist the new "forms of ideological colonization" that destroy the family.

Nova Patria Christi, Africa, Paul VI said; Africa is Christ's new homeland. This statement may remind us of the episode of the flight of the Holy Family into Egypt, when King Herod was seeking to have the Infant Jesus killed. Today, when there are so many Herods, even within the Catholic Church, who relentlessly pursue the family to destroy it, how could the Church in Africa, which has started to build herself up as "God's Family", feel that she is unconcerned? She is more aware than ever of her mission to give refuge to the family and to protect it by committing herself resolutely to accepting fully God's plan for

---

[15]John Paul II, *Letter to Families* (February 2, 1994), 2.

marriage and the family as Christ revealed it to us and as the Church has always taught us. At a time when the Holy Innocents continue to be massacred, she wishes to promote the teaching given by Pope Blessed Paul VI in *Humanae vitae* and updated by Pope Saint John Paul II in *Evangelium vitae*.

As she does so, she is not unaware of the fact that on her own soil some groups are spending billions to promote gender ideology and universal access to "health care" that implies sexual and reproductive "rights" and is now irremediably infected by the perspective of the Western sexual revolution, as though the human person, especially a woman, were some sort of animal. She does not forget that some have tried twice to kill the African family on its own soil: The Cairo Conference[16] and the Maputo Protocol.[17] In welcoming the delegates of the Council of the Bishops' Conferences of Europe (CCEE) in Maputo, of all places, in May 2015, to discuss the theme "The Joy of the Family", the Symposium of Episcopal Conferences of Africa and Madagascar (SECAM) meant to send a strong message to the whole world: "We will not let the family be destroyed!"

In this battle for the faith, Africa knows that it can find refuge and comfort in the palms of the pierced hands of the Crucified Lord, as John Paul II reminded it.[18] This saintly pope showed by his life what it costs disciples of Christ to be committed to defending the family. It is no accident that on the day of the announcement of the creation of the Pontifical Institute for Studies on Marriage and Family he was struck by bullets and collapsed on Saint Peter's Square. In canonizing this pope who was miraculously saved by Our Lady of Fatima—according to his own testimony of faith—during the year in which the long synodal

---

[16]United Nations Organization, International Conference on Population and Development, Cairo, September 5–13, 1994.

[17]African Union, Protocol to the African Charter on Human and Peoples' Rights concerning the rights of women in Africa.

[18]"On account of the many difficulties, crises, and conflicts which bring about so much suffering and misery on the Continent, some Africans are at times tempted to think that the Lord has abandoned them, that he has forgotten them (cf. Is 49:14)! 'And God answers with the words of the great Prophet: "Can a woman forget her own baby and not love the child she bore? Even if a mother should forget a child, I will never forget you. I have written your names on the palms of my hands" (Is 49:15–16). Yes, on the palms of Christ, pierced by the nails of the Crucifixion. The name of each one of you [Africans] is written on those palms. Therefore with full confidence we cry out: "The Lord is our help and our shield. In him do our hearts find joy. We trust in his holy name" (Ps 28:7)'" (John Paul II, *Ecclesia in Africa* 143).

march dedicated to the family began for the Church, cannot the Universal Church that is "God's Family" commit herself resolutely to pursuing this work of defending and promoting the family? Therefore, there is no reason to fear that, as happened to the Crucified Lord, a sword might pierce the hearts of these three Blessed Pontiffs whom the Church raised to the honors of the altar in the year of the Extraordinary Assembly of the Synod of Bishops on the Family because she did not come to the defense of the family.

Nor is there reason to fear, as the Archbishop of Addis-Abeba, Berhaneyesus Cardinal Souraphiel recalled in Accra during the meeting for pastors and theologians organized by SECAM (June 8–12, 2015) to prepare for the next synod, that Saint Charles Lwanga and his Companions, the Martyrs of Uganda, who were canonized by Paul VI, might be driven from the Church because now she had canonized homosexual union, the rejection of which in the name of Jesus was the cause of their martyrdom.

When Pope Benedict XVI said that Africa is a continent of hope, and even the "spiritual lung of humanity", he was in fact pointing out to the Church in Africa her vocation and mission for these difficult times, in which no one dares any more to speak against the dictatorship of relativism, against the pressure of public opinion that no longer believes in anything. From the depths of our African savannas and forests, we can speak, speak clearly, speak forcefully. Yet the word we are trying to make heard is not ours but one that comes to us from God. We wish to lend to this word our voices, which are accustomed to crying out in the desert and in the forests. In their wisdom our elders taught us, when we were children, that, in order to avoid meeting wild beasts in the forest, it is necessary to talk loud, it is necessary to sing along the way, for wild animals flee a path that is frequented by human beings. If along the pathways of the Church the voice of Christ's disciples clearly proclaims the Gospel of the Family, the wild beasts that seek to destroy it will flee, thus preventing families that are already wounded from being finished off by their ferocity.

Out of mercy for these families, the Church in Africa simply wishes to lend her voice to the Gospel of the Family. May the Lord give her the breath and the courage to do so!

Start from Living Faith

An African Take on the *Instrumentum laboris*

Bishop Barthélemy Adoukonou

On June 23, 2015, the General Secretariat of the Synod of Bishops published the *Instrumentum laboris*, which will serve as a basis for discussion at the XIV Ordinary Assembly of the Synod of Bishops scheduled for October 4–25, 2015, concerning the delicate and important question of "the vocation and mission of the family in the Church and the contemporary world". This working document, in keeping with what had been announced in the *Lineamenta* concerning the summary issued by the Extraordinary Assembly of the Synod of Bishops, has retained as a basic component the "text of the *Relatio Synodi* to which a summary of the *Responses, Observations,* and scholarly *Contributions* has been incorporated" (Cardinal Baldisseri, Presentation of the *Instrumentum laboris*). Its three-part structure ("Considering the Challenges of the Family", "The Discernment of the Family Vocation", and "The Mission of the Family Today") was dictated, according to the Cardinal Secretary General, by the concern to maintain continuity between the two synod assemblies.

The first impression that the reader gets from this text is a sense of satisfaction: progress has been made since the close of the extraordinary assembly. The *Relatio synodi* has been enriched by newly contributed material, as the print edition of the *Instrumentum laboris* shows. According to the testimony of the Cardinal General Secretary, ninety-nine responses to the *Lineamenta* have reached the Secretariat of the Synod of Bishops from competent bodies, "359 observations sent freely from dioceses, parishes, ecclesial associations, grass-roots groups of faithful, civil

Bishop Barthélemy Adoukonou is the secretary of the Pontifical Council for Culture.

movements and organizations, numerous families and individual believers". What new material has it contributed? Has it taken into account the critical questions that were left hanging at the end of the extraordinary assembly? How should the *Instrumentum laboris* be received?

1. A Look at the New Contribution of the *Instrumentum laboris*

Part 1, devoted to "Considering the Challenges of the Family", presents some new aspects that were not touched on in the *Lineamenta*. In chapter 1, the document points out the anthropological changes (no. 7) that are observable today: a minority of Christians living according to Church doctrine on marriage and the family, the decreasing number of marriages, the increase in the number of separations and divorces, fear of the young to make definitive commitments, separation between sexuality and procreation. It also notes cultural and social contradictions (nos. 8–9), where contemporary society seems to support the institution of the family while working to weaken it at the same time. Chapter 2, in no. 11, depicts the family as an irreplaceable resource of society before noting the challenges in addition to the challenge of solitude and insecurity considered by the *Relatio synodi*: the economic challenge (no. 14), the challenge of poverty and social exclusion (no. 15), the ecological challenge (no. 16). Chapter 3 integrates elements of the Holy Father's catechesis on the family that look particularly at the elderly (nos. 17–18), widowhood (no. 19), the final stage of life and mourning in the family (no. 20), the handicapped (nos. 21–23). Another aspect—very dear to Pope Francis, as his first pastoral visit (Lampedusa) indicated—is the challenge of migration and its negative effect on the family (nos. 24–27). The role of women is also addressed (no. 3) as well as the bioethical challenge (no. 34).

Part 2 also contributes new elements: natural marriage and sacramental fullness (no. 40), several elements from the catechesis of Pope Francis on marriage and the family: indissolubility, as a gift and a task (no. 42; catechesis of May 6, 2015), living as a family (no. 43; catechesis of May 13, 2015), and conjugal union and fruitfulness (no. 45; catechesis of April 15, 2015), as well as the missionary dimension of the family (no. 48), the family's life of prayer (no. 51), and catechesis and the family (no. 53).

In Part 3, the wedding liturgy is discussed (no. 73). All of chapter 3 is devoted to the accompaniment of the family by the Church, with long expositions on mercy, the way of penance, the preparation of workers, and an increase in the number of ecclesiastical tribunals.

In substance, therefore, the *Instrumentum laboris* enlarges the scope of reflection by offering a framework in which it is more clearly apparent that the theme of the synod is indeed the family and not only a few particular cases, which was the impression left by the extraordinary assembly. Even though we must welcome this considerable effort made during the intersynodal period, a careful reading of the *Instrumentum laboris* nevertheless leaves several points of concern. And since, during the time before the synod assembly, it is our concern to help as best we can to make the Good News of the Family more audible, we will make a few critical comments on the working document submitted to the entire People of God, before indicating the major anthropological place where the thinking would gain much by being deepened in order to ensure a truly effective family ministry.

2. Continuing Presence of the Difficulty Posed by the *Relatio synodi*

In the press conference in which he presented the *Instrumentum laboris*, the Cardinal General Secretary of the Synod of Bishops pointed to the *Relatio synodi* as "a solid point of departure for the path to come". One can well understand the emphasis placed by this affirmation on the link desired by the Holy Father between the two synod sessions. By asking that the text of the *Relatio synodi* be reprinted extensively in the *Lineamenta*, he has in fact wished to indicate to everyone that we are not starting over with a new synod—the next ordinary assembly being completely in continuity with the synodal proceedings begun in October 2014. But one can perhaps be somewhat perplexed by the fact that this text, which was not adopted without difficulty and which did not receive the approval of the Synod Fathers in all points, sent to the People of God as *Lineamenta* and, as such, likely to receive criticism and new contributions, has been simply reproduced in the *Instrumentum laboris*, as if the People had not been involved in the reflection on it. It is thus surprising that the *Instrumentum laboris* has not taken into account the questions that may have been brought up here and there by the particular Churches and all the other ecclesial authorities to whom this text was sent. The "summary of *Responses*, *Observations*, and scholarly *Contributions*" does not, in any case, show this. Unless the *Relatio synodi* did not receive any *modi*. In that case, why then would it have been given as *Lineamenta*?

It is difficult, indeed, to believe that after the lively "debates" of the extraordinary assembly, in which all the Synod Fathers "spoke firmly", "frankly and courageously", without "prior censorship" (these are Pope Francis' words), they did not continue in their local Churches a more in-depth reflection on the points that were central to the lively "debates", which they had, moreover, been asked to do. In fact, "when God's will is sought, in a synod assembly, there are different points of view and there is debate—and this is not a bad thing! Providing it be done with humility and with the spirit of service to the assembly of brothers. Prior censorship would have been a bad thing. No, no, each one had to say what he was thinking" (General Audience, December 10, 2014).

Were the discussions surrounding the *Relatio synodi* closed so that it might be considered a "solid point of departure"? Could the *sensus fidei* of the rest of the People of God who were not at the synod and who had in hand the document as *Lineamenta* say nothing about the controversial points? And if they were able say something, was it not the responsibility of the *Instrumentum laboris* to show this clearly in the spirit of *parrêsia* desired by Pope Francis?

The following observations start from this concern of the Holy Father for a Church that has the "courage of Gospel truth" and from the intention to help, humbly and with a spirit of service, these genuine expectations of the People of God, with their different emphases, really to reach the Supreme Pastor without "prior censorship". In this connection, it seems to us that the *Instrumentum laboris*, which offers numerous positive points that we have highlighted, displays a methodological weakness that we would like now to point out.

3. The Methodological Limitation

The fundamental methodological limitation that we observe in the document lies in the fact that it utilizes the resources of almost all the human and social sciences to put into context the topic of the family today without bringing to light the most important background, namely, the historical choices that led to this disaster. These choices that have been made, not only at the philosophical level, but also and especially at the spiritual and existential levels, strictly speaking, are summed up in man's conscious decision to exclude God from his thinking and from his every-day life. He chose to think about himself and about his relation to the world without God. And so he invented different socio-anthropological, cultural, economic, and political paradigms that, becoming global, are gradually leading to the active destruction of the family.

There are efforts today to impose this sort of option on all the socio-cultural areas where the Church has arisen in recent centuries. But the cultural forms that are encountered in these areas of first evangelization have retained up to now reference to God as a fundamental component. By seeking to impose on them a vision of the world without God, one is in fact exerting an unacceptable symbolic violence on them.

This attempt at "ideological neo-colonization" which Pope Francis has repeatedly denounced must not be buried in the document as though it were a minor news item. In reality, what is at stake is the future of three-quarters of the world's Catholics, who will find themselves in these areas of first evangelization in the next few decades, according to the statistics on the progress of Christianity in the world.[1]

Gathered in synod to discuss such a central topic as the family, the Church owes it to herself to deliver clear words aimed at this great mass of Christians who are striving enthusiastically and joyfully to observe the Gospel requirements as the thing that confers on their humanity its genuine and ultimate meaning. If she failed to do that, she would dangerously compromise the future of Christianity in these regions that are forcefully challenged today not only by a radical, militant Islamism, but also by a certain Western civilization that is secularist, hedonist, sensualist, and consumerist.

The Church in Africa does not forget that it was internal quarreling in the Church along with heresies that precipitated Rome's loss of North Africa (in the seventh to eighth centuries), which was devoured by the barbarous Vandals and Islam. Wounded by that experience, she does not

---

[1] According to this statistical data, in 2010, Europe had only 25.9% of the world's Christians, as opposed to 36.8% in North and South America, 23.6% in sub-Saharan Africa, and 13.1% in Asia and the Pacific. These figures are actually affected by the rate of religious practice, which is relatively weak in the countries of the Northern Hemisphere in comparison to the countries in the South. In 2050, Africa, which will be home to one-quarter of the world's population, will have the highest growth rate for Christianity, if present trends continue. There is reason to fear that the hot spots of Islamic tension in Africa are connected to a strategy to slow the advance of Christianity in Africa. Without getting involved in expansionist competition, this is a fact with which the Church in Africa must cope.

wish to remain silent at a time when Boko Haram[2] is carrying off her daughters by the hundreds, so as to take them away, according to their propaganda, from a civilization with dissolute morals; at a time when the Daesh[3] is seeking to multiply caliphates on its territory, when Aqmi[4] is at work in the Sahel, and other extremist movements seek to set up radical Islamic regimes everywhere, which confuse decadent Western civilization with Christianity. We have the obligation to set ourselves apart from that postmodern civilization, not out of fear or by way of withdrawing into our own enclaves, but out of fidelity to our deep Christian and African identity. For the sake of attracting people, we do not want to put ourselves into situations that would compromise our values, under the illusion of being open to the world in that way.

What Africa perceives along these lines, the Church in Europe should feel even more strongly, on a continent that openly denies its Christian roots and thus provides a fertile breeding ground not only for the radical atheism of postmodernism, but also for a no less radical form of Islamism. In fact, there are young European citizens who go by the hundreds to enlist in the jihadist groups in Syria, Iraq, and Afghanistan or in other countries. These young men certainly do not go there because they are merely poor and unemployed, but above all because Western consumerist society no longer offers them any true values. Everything in it is cheap and banal. Should not such tragic situations prompt us, not to go on a crusade, but to imitate Saint Benedict of Nursia, who, confronted with the decadence of Roman civilization, retired to the "desert" to seek GOD ALONE? The Roman Empire declined—and the present world and its form will pass, too—but the "desert" flowered with monasteries. And starting from those monasteries, European culture was regenerated and European farmlands were cleared. Charlemagne, being a skillful and intelligent statesman, was able to take advantage of this so as to develop the "holy empire" from which medieval Europe was born. If, in the

[2] Boko Haram is a Sunni group that preaches and conducts jihad. Founded in 2002 in Nigeria, it pledged allegiance to the Islamic State (in Arabic: Daesh) on March 7, 2015, and has become the "West African Province" thereof.

[3] Daesh: from the Arabic acronym meaning "Islamic State", which is an armed Islamist organization, Salafist and jihadist in its ideology, that was founded in Iraq around the year 2006.

[4] Aqmi: Al-Quaida in Islamic Maghreb, which has distinguished itself especially in the war in Mali.

current crisis of civilization, the Church truly goes to God first, people will flock to her, and a true civilization based on a culture of life will flourish. The family will live, will be proclaimed as Good News, and will itself become an evangelizer.

Consequently, the *Instrumentum laboris* ought to have been fundamentally a call to the Church in all socio-cultural areas to tell us how the institution of the family appears in those spaces. This uplifting of voices from the various peripheries, as though in a video feedback, would not fail to show the European Church that evangelized them the horrors of the anthropology that currently prevails on its territory. It would also make manifest the paradoxical position in which the West finds itself today, with a godless anthropology that raises a hue and cry demanding that the Church align her doctrine with its unacceptable requirements. The Church in the West would understand then that she should not agree to think of her pastoral practice in terms of such an anthropology. It is not possible for her to "inculturate" marriage and the family on a basis that has, in fact, proved to be destructive of fundamental human goods. The culture conversion required of the Young Churches that face traditional cultures is necessary more than ever here, too, in the Western world. And the only way to do this is to call into question fundamentally the exclusion of God. Now this is precisely what some people, even in the Church, do not have the courage to do or seem unwilling to do; unfortunately, the text of the *Instrumentum laboris* seems to show traces of this reluctance in some passages.

Today we hear Church leaders in the West say that "our family model is not universal"—which means that we must not make it into an absolute—at the very moment when some pagan human societies recognize monogamy as the norm in their cultural documents and consider their polygamous practices to be a deviation that is only tolerated. One can understand, therefore, why eminent Western anthropological researchers seek to distort traditional cultural practices among so-called "primitive" peoples so as to find in them foundations for homosexual unions.[5]

---

[5] Françoise Héritier, who succeeded Claude Lévi-Strauss at the Collège de France, in an article written for the *Encyclopaedia universalis*, presents two social institutions in which she thinks she has found signs of socially recognized unions of persons of the same sex. One of the examples was taken from the Yoruba world that we know well. Yoruba merchant women who pay the bride-price of girls promised in marriage do not become their partners but, on the contrary, exempt them from a forced or premature marriage, giving them the opportunity to mature before marrying a man of their choice.

To counteract these "outside" anthropologies, which are a form of "neocolonial" manipulation (to use Pope Francis' expression), the wise men of the various cultural areas of the world, if they are organized and structured by the Church into genuine groups of missionary research, will be able to place at her disposal the rich cultural patrimony of the peoples that, purified and illumined by the Gospel, could restore to our world, which has lost its meaning, its humanity as well. In these cultural areas, God has remained structurally present in the cultures, despite the violence inflicted on them by a certain modern anthropological scholarship by seeking to suppress in its published works any reference to God found in them.[6] These cultures exhibit forms of the family that certainly have problems but do not dispute the profound nature of the family, which springs from the marriage of a man and a woman, in their sexual diversity and complementarity. Is this not what anthropology had already firmly established before postmodern gender ideology?

If that is the case, it seems to us that the synod is bound to invite the Church from the different socio-cultural and geo-anthropological areas to reclassify all the "wounds" suffered by the family about which the *Instrumentum laboris* speaks so much, so as to interpret them clearly as consequences resulting from the exclusion of God and from a determination to design a new type of man according to the good pleasure of the committed atheist that postmodern man claims to be. These are the wounds that make up the extreme malaise of which the families of the world can be healed only by conversion from precisely the sort of sin that is at the origins of postmodernity. This movement, if we can put it this way, wishes to kill mercy itself and the Holy Spirit who inspires it. But did the Lord not say that if someone sins against the Holy Spirit, he will never be forgiven? Therefore, we must not be complacent about the "original sin of postmodernity". We must be converted to God and ask the world to convert to God's mercy. It seems to us there is no other way.

It is necessary then, we think, to make a diagnosis clearly by region. If the illness from which mankind is suffering is not diagnosed correctly,

---

[6] It is well known that Gaston Fessard had written to Lévi-Strauss to ask him why he had taken the liberty to delete the reference to the supernatural in the French translation of his research report on the Amazon Basin that he had first presented in English. This report also included a clear mention of the supernatural. The structuralist scholar gave him no answer. See the posthumous work *La dialectique des exercices spirituels de St Ignace*, vol. 3, ed. Michel Sales (Paris: Lethielleux, 1984). The reader may also refer to Frédéric Louzeau, *L'Anthropologie sociale du Père Gaston Fessard* (Paris: PUF, 2009).

we cannot prescribe the appropriate treatment. This diagnosis depends on the locality: a headache is not a sprained ankle, even though the pain caused by either one is felt throughout the body. Although all mankind is sick, the ailments of the West are not exactly the same as those of Asia or Africa. But unless all work together to treat them, no part of the body will be at rest. In the case of a cancerous tumor, there would even be a risk of metastasis. This is the danger to which mankind is exposed today. It is necessary to prevent the metastasis of radical atheism and its anthropological consequences.

Conscious more than ever of this interdependence, Africa would like to remind the Church in the West that she could not possibly engage in a hermetically sealed dialogue with the postmodern world, while ridiculing other countries as though they were trapped in various forms of obscurantism that no one understands, without seriously compromising her faith and Christian roots. She could not do so by appealing to God's mercy, while in fact she would be sacrificing all the other cultures that are still open to God and susceptible to authentic inculturation, understood as the acceptance of the grace of redemption that is a sacrament.

The Church in Africa, committed since Easter of 1994 to building herself up as the Family of God, strives to conduct a work of inculturation for the benefit of the Universal Church, for which the acceptance by a plurality of the notion of family found in pleas on behalf of the divorced and remarried or, worse yet, on behalf of homosexual unions is totally unacceptable because it is scandalous, even in the view of pagans and of morally upright atheists, who are astonished by certain "politically correct" proposals of Church leaders, which add to the confusion because they lack evangelical clarity and "parrêsia".

4. Some Rather Unclear Formulations

The confusion that is quite evident in some sections and paragraphs could well express a lack of transparency with regard to the theological criterion of inculturating the faith in the modern context. In the case of the ancient world, Saint Paul already honestly acknowledged the failure of an approach to inculturation that started from the culture and then ascended to the Christian principle (see Acts 17:22–32, the discourse in the Areopagus); if so, then we have a right to ask whether the working document is truly aware of the contradiction that would be entailed in trying to start from a deliberately atheistic culture, such as the postmodern secularist culture of the West today, and claiming to arrive at Christianity from there. Saint Paul, in any case, admitted his mistake and declared in Corinth that in any future work of inculturation he would start only from the Christian principle, the most eloquent expression of which is the Crucified Lord: "I did not come proclaiming to you the testimony of God in lofty words or wisdom. For I decided to know nothing among you except Jesus Christ and him crucified" (1 Cor 2:1–2). By starting from him, the Lord of Glory, Paul was able to recognize in the Hellenistic culture to which he belonged what the Fathers of the Church later called "seeds of the Word", "favorable conditions", and "preparations for the Gospel".

Wherever the document depicts the Gospel as a burden or an inaccessible ideal, it is impossible for it to point to it as the final goal toward which we would like to lead so-called "cultural values" that are described, in an astonishing rhetorical turn, as "seeds of the Word" (no. 99). An anthropology rooted in an obligatory atheism will never be able to arrive at the New Man that Christ represents.

The document goes on at length about topics such as homosexuality, gender, and the divorced and remarried and sprinkles them with "values" that are proclaimed nominally and presented as "seeds of the Word", which is quite obviously a contradiction. All the obscurity and confusion follow from this.

The Synod Fathers, therefore, have to state clearly that for the Christian faith there is no inculturation unless it takes into account the necessity of conversion. And if even the cultures that have not excluded God feel the need to convert—and they must—all the more so should those cultures built in opposition to God, because the mercy that Christ offers us is all concentrated in his glorious Cross. You will not find it anywhere else.

On the basis of these brief reflections on the criteria for inculturation, *let us read, for example, section 8.*

Whereas the document seeks to point out cultural contradictions, it ends up in logical contradictions itself:

> The resulting confusion is of no assistance in defining the specific character of such [intimate] unions in society. Rather, it relegates the special bond between biological difference, reproduction, and human identity

to an individualistic choice. What is certainly needed is a more thorough examination of human nature and culture which is based not simply on biology and sexual difference, fully aware that "the removal of differ- ence [...] creates a problem, not a solution" (Francis, *General Audience*, April 15, 2015).

We find here three levels of ambiguity. The most subtle, it seems to us, is resorting to a quotation by Pope Francis to defend a choice that the text of the document would seem to urge the Synod Fathers to make, by relativizing a more in-depth examination of the sexual difference at the biological level and favoring chiefly an examination of it at the cultural level, as gender theory intends to do. Proceeding in this way assures gen- der theoreticians of the at least partial agreement of the Synod Fathers. It is necessary to expose this subterfuge and prevent it from becoming a point of consensus of the Synod Fathers. We cannot in any way give our assent to this theory that seeks to contradict God on the very ground of his act of creating man. How pretentious to try to substitute cultural sexuality for the biological sexuality inscribed by God himself in the human being as a principle of differentiation and complementarity! And how could so important a document as an *Instrumentum laboris* allow this serious vagueness, in blatant contradiction to the words of the pope that are cited?

The second level of chiaroscuro is the generalization to all socio- cultural contexts worldwide of a phenomenon that pertains only to a very small part of mankind: the West and, within it, a minority of activist ideologues whom more serious scholars describe as "scientific proselytes".

In the same document, finally, it is difficult to distinguish observation from analysis. One can retort that sections 7 and 8 are in part 1, which is dedicated to "listening" and considering. But then why announce that a "more thorough examination" should be made, to which the other parts of the document make no further reference at all?

Further illustrations

As for section 22, which deals with the challenge of handicaps, we read:

> Some ardently desire that, in a truly welcoming community, the family
> and the person with special needs will not feel alone and rejected, but

might find relief and support, especially when the family's strength and resources are lacking.

It is surprising that such a recommendation is not made also with regard to the divorced and civilly remarried, for whom the document argues in favor of Eucharistic Communion. The handicapped persons mentioned in section 22 already receive sacramental Communion, and yet they suffer from isolation. This, then, is because Eucharistic Communion has no magical power to relieve us of loneliness. Therefore, it seem to us pastorally urgent to have the entire Church benefit from the prodigious light that comes to us from the theologian Henri de Lubac, who tells us that, until the Middle Ages, the expression "Mystical Body" designated the Eucharist and that the *res* of the *sacramentum* (in other words, what the sacramental sign points to) was the ecclesial community as "the real body of Christ". Besides the spiritual communion that Pope Benedict XVI discussed so well, perhaps it would be just as important for our pastoral practice to aim at reviving a spirituality of the "fraternal body of Christ" in order to respond to the need for closeness suffered by our divorced and remarried brethren, whom some would like to admit to the Eucharistic Body of Christ despite the organic connection that exists between the sacraments. We must unceasingly learn to be Church and to live fraternally with all our brothers and sisters, even those who are in a situation objectively contrary to God's will.

The last paragraph of section 30

Speaking about the role of women, the document says:

> A contributing factor in acknowledging the determining role of women in society could be a greater appreciation of their responsibility in the Church, namely, their involvement in the decision-making process, their participation—not simply in a formal way—in the governing of some institutions; and their involvement in the formation of ordained ministers.

In a document like this *Instrumentum laboris*, in which the Church aims to focus the pastoral concern of the bishops on the Good News of the Family, who can miss the fact that the mention of the serious problem of the role of women in the Church is out of place here? It will never be too late for the Church to call a synod on that topic, but here it seems to us better not to mix problems and, therefore, purely and simply to delete this paragraph!

Bioethical challenge: sections 34–35

In section 34, we find an expression, or its equivalent, that recurs often in the text: "different situations", "a variety of situations" (35), or the like. Such formulas are the quintessential expression of the confusion that is liable to lead the Fathers astray in their discernment. What clarity are they trying to bring to these Fathers, who have assembled precisely so as to be able to make decisions about well-circumscribed realities, as we see in section 36 in the request received by the General Secretariat of the Synod for a more precise definition of the category of those who are "far from the Church".

In section 42, second paragraph, we read:

> The Gospel of the Family offers an ideal in life which must take into account a sense of the times and the real difficulties in permanently maintaining commitments. In this regard, the Church needs to proclaim a message which might give hope and not be burdensome, so that every family may know that the Church never abandons the family, because of "the indissoluble bond of the history of Christ and his Church with the history of marriage and the human family" (Francis, *General Audience*, May 6, 2015).

The way in which the document describes the difficulty that our contemporaries have in making definitive commitments gives the painful impression that the Gospel in itself is a burden from which the Church, out of mercy, ought to strive to relieve our poor contemporaries. Such an idea is basically unacceptable, because it would mean accusing God of putting a crushing burden on the shoulders of modern man. Can the Church be so pretentious as to think that she is more merciful than her Lord and God? The young people who are supposed to be crushed by the Church's "moralism" nevertheless prove capable of radically committing their lives to unfortunate ventures like terrorism. Why would the young people in our Christian families not also be capable of definitive commitments, without which one cannot form a family? Inviting the young to a "sursum corda" should not be synonymous with "oppression".

In sections 60–65, we find several formulations that, in our opinion, are not helpful, either, to the Synod Fathers in their discernment. Section 60, for example, starts with a very felicitous formulation of the mission of the family, which is followed immediately by a plea that seems to claim to have greater importance than what was just stated; a plea that is supported by a quotation from the pope.

> 60. *The Church, a sure teacher and caring mother, recognizes that the only marriage bond for those who are baptized is sacramental and any breach of it is against the will of God. At the same time, the Church is conscious of the weakness of many of her children who are struggling in their journey of faith. "Consequently, without detracting from the evangelical ideal, they need to accompany with mercy and patience the eventual stages of personal growth as these progressively occur.... A small step in the midst of great human limitations can be more pleasing to God than a life which outwardly appears in order and passes the day without confronting great difficulties. Everyone needs to be touched by the comfort and attraction of God's saving love, which is mysteriously at work in each person, above and beyond their faults and failings"* (Evangelii gaudium 44).

An effort to identify and spell out the ways in which the Church, through parents as well as through priests and other pastoral workers, should carry out her mission of education and evangelization seems to us to be the real, concrete way of practicing mercy. Effective dedication to the accompaniment of young people spiritually on their path of conversion and filial relationship with God seems to us to be such a practical exercise of mercy.

What we find in section 61 seems by no means capable of enlightening the Synod Fathers. This section asserts that the family "is not a duty but a gift", without explaining whether we are considering baptized persons or non-Christians. To speak then about the sacrament of marriage as the object of a "decision" and as a "goal to be achieved" seems confused, and the process of maturation that leads to it is even more so. With all these imprecise expressions, the document again seeks to weaken the capacity for discernment of the one who welcomes the couple in question by attributing to him a Pharisaical attitude against which it warns: "It is important to be clearly aware that everyone is weak and that each person is a sinner like everyone else, yet not failing to affirm the blessings and values of a Christian marriage" (61). When all is said and done, at what is this aiming?

As for section 68, which correctly discusses mercy as "revealed truth", it seems to us important to emphasize once again that in the cases highlighted by the *Instrumentum laboris* it is not so much a matter of recalling the doctrine of God's mercy as of clearly discerning the categories of persons who actually turn to this divine mercy and of describing the way in which the Church should help them do so. Therefore, we will have to continue to be careful about the way in which we speak about mercy. Some formulations seem to be written in the key of "rights to be claimed"—just as in the United Nations they claim rights for this minority or that category of persons. Can we claim God's mercy? A real change of mind-set has to be made here: the real conversion needed by our age of general commitment to the triumph of individualistic rights in order to become an age of personalistic commitment to recognizing duty. We turn humbly to God's mercy, and we work to be more open to it in truth. And this is where the Church, as a compassionate Mother, accompanies us, since she herself is humbly the sacrament of this mercy, as Pope Francis invites her to be in *Misericordiae vultus*.

Section 81 of the document reads:

> In light of the Word of God, which requires discernment in various situations, pastoral care ought to take into consideration the need of communicating with others in a manner open to dialogue and free from prejudice, especially in cases where Catholics, in matters of marriage and family life, do not live or are in no condition to live in full accord with the Church's teaching.

In order to dispel the impression that we have here a ready-made discernment to which the document wishes to lead others, it seems necessary to recall once and for all that the only clear-sighted person is the one who is himself in a state of humble conversion, authentically open to the light of the Holy Spirit, which is none other than the Spirit of the Crucified Lord. Is this really the attitude of discernment that runs through the whole text of the *Instrumentum laboris*? Or is it another attitude, and if so, by what spirit is it inspired?

In section 98 we read:

> *While continuing to proclaim and foster Christian marriage, the Synod also encourages pastoral discernment of the situations of a great many who no longer live this reality. Entering into pastoral dialogue with these persons is needed to distinguish*

elements in their lives that can lead to a greater openness to the Gospel of Marriage in its fullness. Pastors ought to identify elements that can foster evangelization and human and spiritual growth. A new element in today's pastoral activity is a sensitivity to the positive aspects of civilly celebrated marriages and, with obvious differences, cohabitation. While clearly presenting the Christian message, the Church also needs to indicate the constructive elements in these situations that do not yet or no longer correspond to it.

Has this new sensitivity that is supposedly part of pastoral practice today itself been discerned in the light of the Spirit of the Crucified that we just mentioned, or is it a norm derived from the formatting of postmodern man, who, as we know, is determined to fight against God? It is astonishing that this section, which is a repeat of section 41 of the *Relatio synodi*, should be reprinted here as though self-evident. It contains elements that are highly debatable and even in contradiction with Catholic doctrine. We emphasize that such a formulation could have been avoided while preserving the pastoral concern for closeness that obviously drives its authors. In order to do that, it would have been enough to end the passage at the words "human and spiritual growth":

> While continuing to proclaim and foster Christian marriage, the Synod also encourages pastoral discernment of the situations of a great many who no longer live this reality. Entering into pastoral dialogue with these persons is needed to distinguish elements in their lives that can lead to a greater openness to the Gospel of Marriage in its fullness. Pastors ought to identify elements that can foster evangelization and human and spiritual growth. ~~A new element in today's pastoral activity is a sensitivity to the positive aspects of civilly celebrated marriages and, with obvious differences, cohabitation. While clearly presenting the Christian message, the Church also needs to indicate the constructive elements in these situations that do not yet or no longer correspond to it.~~

Indeed, what need would there be to keep the rest of the section, if not to affirm a "new sensitivity" that is now normative, recognizing "positive aspects" in sinful situations? Are the divorced and remarried and cohabiting couples the ones who are asking the Church to give a description of their life-styles? Why this insistence on finding "positive aspects" in their situation?

Section 99, which is a commentary on the preceding section, need not recommend finding "seeds of the Word" in cohabitation, either.

This passage retains all its value, provided we delete from it the expressions "in a gradual discovery of 'the seeds of the Word' which lie hidden, so as to value them" and "the fullness of". The corrected section would read as follows:

> Since the Sacrament of Matrimony is an indissoluble and exclusively faithful union between a man and a woman who are called to receive one another and welcome life, Christian marriage is a great grace for the human family. The Church has the duty and the mission to proclaim this grace to each person in every circumstance. The Church also ought to accompany those in a civil marriage or those living together ~~in a gradual discovery of "the seeds of the Word" which lie hidden, so as to value them~~ until ~~the fullness of~~ union in the Sacrament might be achieved.

Section 100 mentions a concept of marriage in stages, which is thought to be customary in Africa; some wish to take this as their inspiration in the postmodern Western context with its "new pastoral sensitivity". In reply, it is important to note that, as early as the 1980s, particularly careful anthropological research made it possible to dismiss this concept of marriage, which was erroneously thought to be typical of Africa. What we know about African traditions strongly resembles Jewish traditions, in which betrothals have the "legal status" of a stage before marriage (as was the case with Joseph and Mary). But this stage ruled out any common life. Not until the wedding day is the marriage consummated; and the next day the parents come to receive proudly and happily the signs testifying to their daughter's virginity. There is no analogy between this traditional system and modern forms of cohabitation, all the more so because the traditional family never recognizes any other marriage for its daughter who is lawfully married in a first wedding and for whom, together with the ancestors themselves, it received the bride-price. The ceremony has a sacred character, and for this very reason the marriage is unique and indissoluble.

Section 108, §2, asks the Church to show respect and mercy toward "those who have failed in marriage", just as she asks divorced persons to do in their relations with one another. We wonder: What Church is meant here? The hierarchy or the ecclesial, diocesan, or parish community? In both cases, it will be necessary to avoid treating divorced persons as being outside the Church. The absolute respect that is due to every person does not include leaving him a slave to sin through a supposed respect for his personal condition.

Section 112 is a repetition without commentary of section 47 of the *Lineamenta*. Along with no. 113, it is one of the rare passages to make explicit and rather detailed mention of those who have remained faithful to the marital bond, despite separation. They deserve, as no. 113 stresses, "acknowledgment and support from the Church, which must reveal to them the face of a God who never abandons anyone and is always ready to restore strength and hope". It is regrettable, however, that the document does not speak about their situation as extensively as it does about "those who have failed in marriage" and have civilly entered another conjugal union or are cohabiting.

Who experiences in their flesh the burden of loneliness more than separated married persons who nevertheless have remained faithful to the bond? It is truly astonishing that the document was so circumspect about them. Why this stinginess with attention and mercy in their regard?

The two sections 122 and 123 in their entirety give the impression that a connection exists between the non-admission of the divorced and remarried to Eucharistic Communion and the great sufferings that are said to result from it for the children. If these divorced and civilly remarried cannot free themselves from this new bond because of moral obligations toward the children born of their union, can any way be recommended to them other than that prescribed by *Familiaris consortio* 84? If exceptional cases are already recognized and the documents regulating them exist, we do not see the reason why some would like to give special authority to a "delegated priest" (123) who after his evaluation could "bind" or "loose", that is, "dissolve". What would one wish to dissolve? A valid marriage? Would the irreversibility of separation have the power to invalidate the marriage?

3. Proposal for Regrouping Chapters

As for regrouping certain parts of the *Instrumentum laboris*, which would lend more force to the message of the family as a place in which the Triune God is revealed, we propose the following: in adopting the essential material in chapter 4 from part 3, we could place it immediately after chapter 2 from that same part. In that way, it would be easier to show the married couple's cooperation with God in bringing a new human being into existence, which does not stop at the merely physical level, but continues through the parents' participation in giving birth to the human being as a spiritual and moral entity. The first years of a human being's life until adolescence are a unique time for accompanying the child spiritually in listening to God's voice, which resounds in his interior sanctuary and tells him, "do this; avoid that", and rewards him with pure joy when he proves to be docile to that voice. The voice of conscience (*synderesis*) is irreplaceable for every human being, who must become a moral being precisely on the basis of this dialogue with God. Parents are, in this sense, genuinely co-creators insofar as they accompany the arrival of the human being at this primordial level. This is the reason why some African peoples say that parents are co-creators (Mε to nyi Sε, Mε no nyi Sε).

If we were allowed to rearrange these chapters and everyone agreed to reinterpret in this way how a new human being comes about, it would lead to calling into question the way in which the very text of the underlying document proceeds when it tells the reader in several passages to beware of norms and statements about duty. The type of man that the anthropology at work in the document seems to propose as the basis for the inculturation of the family today does not really seem to be in keeping with the mystery of man that Vatican II discussed, especially in section 22 of *Gaudium et spes*.

Conclusion

Divine Providence willed that the Gospel that will be read in churches throughout the world on the day when the XIV Ordinary Assembly of the Synod of Bishops opens will be precisely the one in which the Lord proclaims: "What God has joined, let not man put asunder" (Mk 10:9)! We pray that the synod will welcome this message and will be faithful to it in its work.

The wisdom of the peoples of Africa, which we have mentioned more than once in this brief survey of the *Instrumentum laboris*, despite its limitations, had already held in great esteem the marriage of the first wedding as a divine institution. For this reason, this wisdom considers it unique and indissoluble. Since our efforts for the inculturation of marriage and the family in Africa are devoted to collecting these authentic "seeds of the Word", it is surprising for us to see that nowadays some are trying to find, without previous conversion, "preparations for the

Gospel" in the anthropology of a civilization that has resolutely turned its back on God. If it has rejected God and Jesus Christ, can we still speak logically about "seeds of the Word"? Pastors and theologians are obliged, in our opinion, to give public explanations on these points to all the Synod Fathers, so that their interventions are not made against the background of this serious ambiguity.

For our part, it seems to us absolutely indispensable that we reaffirm the need for a spirit of discernment that allows itself to be enlightened by the mystery of the Cross, which, itself, discerns spirits (cf. 1 Jn 4; 2 Cor 3:17). This spirit and it alone must be applied in order to arrive at a responsible pastoral interpretation of the *Instrumentum laboris*. It will make it possible to clear up all the confusion and to dismiss any alleged "new pastoral sensitivity" whose Christian criteria for validity are unknown.

We hope that the modest contributions made by this book by African pastors collaborating with the pope—some in the Curia, others in the dioceses on the African Continent—might be of some usefulness for future Synod Fathers and more broadly for the whole People of God to whom the *Instrumentum laboris* was sent. These essays will certainly clarify several concrete cases that concern all the pastors who are gathered, not only for a necessary proclamation of the family as Good News, but also in order to care for, heal, and take to heart many sorts of families in distress.

Part Two

The Gospel of the Family

The Importance of Recent Magisterial Teaching on Marriage and the Family

Archbishop Denis Amuzu-Dzakpah

Introduction

If Scripture is the revelation that tradition conveys, if both of them are the rule of the Magisterium, then the latter interprets Scripture and witnesses to tradition. Without this profound unity that makes them absolutely interdependent, Scripture would run the risk of being a dead letter, tradition of being a debatable choice, and the Magisterium of being man's arbitrary interference in the mysteries of God.... If the Magisterium is an authority received from Christ, it is entirely at the service of the word of God, entirely inspired by the love of God. Assisted by the Holy Spirit, it preserves, protects, and explains revelation. Christ continues to teach through it in order to uphold, deepen, and spread the faith among men.[1]

In short, the Magisterium is the power that Christ conferred on the Church to teach and interpret his message authoritatively and certainly. The duty of the Magisterium is, first and foremost, to preserve faithfully and to hand on in its integrity the truth that the Church received from Jesus Christ, her Head and Teacher.

Since the close of the Second Vatican Ecumenical Council, in other words, for more than *fifty years*, the Church has not failed to offer her constant teaching on marriage and the family. One of the most exalted expressions of this recent Magisterium was proposed by the Pastoral Constitution on the Church in the Modern World (*Gaudium et spes*),

Archbishop Denis Amuzu-Dzakpah is the archbishop of Lomé.
[1] Gervais, Dumeige, introduction, *La Foi catholique* (Paris: Éditions de l'Orante, 1969), ix.

which devotes a whole chapter to promoting the dignity of marriage and the family (nos. 47–52). The summary discussion of this theme pertaining to "the importance of recent Magisterial teaching on marriage and family" could be subdivided as follows:

- *From Vatican Council II to* Humanae vitae;
- *From Saint John Paul II to Pope Francis;*
- *Toward a new culture of human life.*

1. From Vatican Council II to *Humanae vitae*

a. The Church in today's world

The Second Vatican Ecumenical Council plainly described marriage as a profound community of life and love (see *Gaudium et spes* 48, §1), placing love at the center of the family and at the same time showing the truth of this love as opposed to various forms of reductionism present in contemporary culture. "Authentic married love" (*Gaudium et spes* 48) implies mutual self-giving and includes and integrates the sexual dimension and affectivity, in keeping with the divine plan. Moreover, the Pastoral Constitution on the Church in the Modern World itself strongly emphasizes that the spouses are rooted in Christ. Yes, Christ the Lord "comes into the lives of married Christians through the sacrament of marriage", and he remains with them so that, "as he loved the Church and handed Himself over on her behalf, the spouses may love each other with perpetual fidelity through mutual self-bestowal" (*Gaudium et spes* 48, §2). In the Incarnation, he takes up human love, purifies it, and leads it to its fullness, and he gives to the spouses, together with his Spirit, the ability to live it by imbuing their whole life with faith, hope, and charity. In this way, spouses are, so to speak, consecrated, and by a specific grace they build up the Body of Christ and form a "domestic church" (see *Lumen gentium* 11).

The procreation and upbringing of children connected with the fertility of marriage neither exclude nor reduce the value of the other ends, especially mutual love. As coworkers and interpreters of God's creative love, spouses are called to practice responsible parenthood. It is up to them to decide, in conformity with divine law, the number of children to whom they will hand on the gift of life. Vatican Council II emphasizes:

Spouses should be aware that they cannot proceed arbitrarily, but must always be governed according to a conscience dutifully conformed to the divine law itself, and should be submissive toward the Church's teaching office, which authentically interprets that law in the light of the Gospel.[2]

b. Toward the responsible regulation of births

In the wake of the Second Vatican Ecumenical Council, the papal Magisterium examined the doctrine on marriage and the family in greater depth. At the request of *Blessed Paul VI*, the difficult question of the regulation of births was studied from *1965* on by a commission of experts that provided a report with a wealth of information and criteria for reaching a solution. After studying this extremely valuable report very carefully, Paul VI courageously took his position. On *July 25, 1968*, he published the famous encyclical *Humanae vitae* on the regulation of births. It is still a good idea and very beneficial to read or reread *Humanae vitae* calmly, so as not to summarize this important encyclical gloomily in these four words: "No to the Pill"! Intellectual honesty cannot allow such lamentable reductionism, which impoverishes thought. The rich teaching of Paul VI on the regulation of births begins with these words: "The transmission of human life is a most serious role in which married people collaborate freely and responsibly with God the Creator. It has always been a source of great joy to them, even though it sometimes entails many difficulties and hardships."[3]

Before setting forth the doctrinal principles that aim to highlight the close connection between conjugal love and the transmission of life, "the great helmsman of Vatican Council II" made sure to situate the problem within an overall vision of mankind: "The question of human procreation, like every other question which touches human life, involves more than ... limited aspects.... It is the whole man and the whole mission to which he is called that must be considered: both its natural, earthly aspects and its supernatural, eternal aspects" (HV 7).

He declares that, because of the respect due to the integrity of the human body and its functions, "the direct interruption of the generative process already begun and, above all, direct abortion, even for therapeutic reasons, are to be absolutely excluded as lawful means of regulating

---

[2] *Gaudium et spes* 50, §2.
[3] *Humanae vitae* 1.

the number of children" (HV 14, §1). "Similarly excluded is any action which either before, at the moment of, or after sexual intercourse is specifically intended to prevent procreation—whether as an end or as a means" (HV 14, §2).

Why, then, the prohibition of these means of birth control? In defending in this way conjugal morality as a whole,

> the Church is convinced that she is contributing to the creation of a truly human civilization. She urges man not to betray his personal responsibilities by putting all his faith in technical expedients. In this way she defends the dignity of husband and wife. This course of action shows that the Church, loyal to the example and teaching of the divine Savior, is sincere and unselfish in her regard for men whom she strives to help even now during this earthly pilgrimage "to share God's life as sons of the living God, the Father of all men".[4]

In these pastoral instructions, Paul VI again calls the attention of educators and of all those who hold positions of responsibility for the common good of society to "the need to create an atmosphere favorable to the growth of chastity so that true liberty may prevail over license and the norms of the moral law be fully safeguarded" (HV 22). He strongly recommends that priests follow the example of the Lord himself, who was "bitterly severe toward sin, but patient and abounding in mercy towards sinners. Husbands and wives, therefore, when deeply distressed by reason of the difficulties of their life, must find stamped in the heart and voice of their priest the likeness of the voice and the love of our Redeemer" (HV 29, §1–2). "Teach married couples the necessary way of prayer and prepare them to approach more often with great faith the Sacraments of the Eucharist and of Penance. Let them never lose heart because of their weakness" (HV 29, §3).

2. From Saint John Paul II to Pope Francis

a. With Saint John Paul II

Saint John Paul II devoted very particular attention to the family through his series of catecheses on human love, his Letter to Families

---

[4]Ibid. 18, §3, citing *Populorum progressio* 21.

(*Gratissimam sane*), dated February 2, 1994, and especially with the apostolic exhortation *Familiaris consortio*, dated November 22, 1981. In these extremely valuable documents, he described the family as the "voice of the Church"; thus he offered an overall vision of man's and woman's vocation to love; he set out the main lines of pastoral care to the family and of the presence of the family in society.

In the introduction to *Familiaris consortio* we read:

> Knowing that marriage and the family constitute one of the most precious of human values, the Church wishes to speak and offer her help to those who are already aware of the value of marriage and the family and seek to live it faithfully, to those who are uncertain and anxious and searching for the truth, and to those who are unjustly impeded from living freely their family lives.[5]

It goes without saying that a correct rereading of the apostolic exhortation *Familiaris consortio* would be, among other things, a beneficial preparation for the next session of the ordinary synod of bishops scheduled for *October 4–25, 2015.*

Taking a closer look, three main ideas seem to emerge from this important apostolic exhortation by Saint John Paul II:

- Called into existence by love, the human being, whoever he may be and whatever he may be, is called to love. Love indisputably remains the first word and the final word of human existence. Love is the reason for being and for living that is written on the very heart of the human being, who is first and foremost a person, that is to say, a being capable of being loved and of loving, capable of mutual, total self-giving. To sum it all up, "Love is ... the fundamental and innate vocation of every human being" (*Familiaris consortio* 11, §2).
- In the experience of family, man is called to live and accomplish in a privileged way this fundamental vocation to love.... This community of persons is the primary cell of society, in which man finds his roots, the place where he originally lives and flourishes, the point at which he is inserted into the human family and into the family of the Church.

[5] *Familiaris consortio* 1, §2.

- This vision of man—and therefore of the family that is connected with him—is based on the biblical, Christian faith in a God who created man "in his image" and who "in Himself ... lives a mystery of personal loving communion".[6]

Part 3 of the apostolic exhortation *Familiaris consortio* explained the duties of the family, a community of life and love, through the four following tasks:

- the formation of a community of persons characterized by the inseparable unity of conjugal communion, indissoluble communion, and care for the child, even before his birth, from the first moment of his conception, and then over the course of his childhood and adolescence;
- service to life by the transmission of life (an invaluable gift from God) and also by the task of education that belongs first to the parents;
- participation in the development of society: "The Christian family is thus called upon to offer everyone a witness of generous and disinterested dedication to social matters, through a 'preferential option' for the poor and disadvantaged" (*Familiaris consortio* 47, §3);
- participation in the life and mission of the Church by a commitment to be a community that believes and evangelizes, a community in dialogue with God and a community in service to mankind.

As for pastoral care to the family in difficult cases, particularly divorced persons who have remarried civilly, Saint John Paul II advised careful discernment of different situations. He recommended encouraging the divorced and remarried "to listen to the word of God, to attend the Sacrifice of the Mass, to persevere in prayer, to contribute to works of charity and to community efforts in favor of justice, to bring up their children in the Christian faith, to cultivate the spirit and practice of penance and thus implore, day by day, God's grace."[7] In any case, even though she cannot admit them to Eucharistic Communion, the Church

[6] Ibid. 11, §2.
[7] Ibid. 84, §3.

will pray for them, will encourage them, and will prove to be for them a merciful Mother concerned about sustaining them in faith and hope.

Finally, in returning to the forceful message of the encyclical *Evangelium vitae* (*March 25, 1995*), it is good to recall that the family ("the sanctuary of life") fulfills its mission of proclaiming the Gospel of Life above all by bringing up children.

> By word and example, in the daily round of relations and choices, and through concrete actions and signs, parents lead their children to authentic freedom, actualized in the sincere gift of self, and they cultivate in them respect for others, a sense of justice, cordial openness, dialogue, generous service, solidarity, and all the other values which help people to live life as a gift. (*Evangelium vitae* 92, §4)

b. With Benedict XVI and Pope Francis

Benedict XVI, in his very first encyclical, *Deus Caritas est* (*God Is Love*), dated *December 25, 2005*, returned to the theme of the truth of the love between man and woman, which, basically, is fully explained only in the light of the love of Christ Crucified (cf. *Deus Caritas est* 2). In it he states in particular that "marriage based on exclusive and definitive love becomes the icon of the relationship between God and his people and vice versa. God's way of loving becomes the measure of human love."[8]

Elsewhere, in his encyclical *Caritas in Veritate* (*Charity in Truth*), dated *June 29, 2009*, he highlights the importance of love as a principle of life in society.[9]

Addressing the theme of the family in the post-synodal apostolic exhortation *Africae munus* (*Africa's commitment*), Benedict XVI teaches us that the family is "the best setting for learning and applying the culture of forgiveness, peace, and reconciliation".[10] And citing in support of this his message for the *2008* World Day of Peace, he reminds us that

> "In a healthy family life we experience some of the fundamental elements of peace: justice and love between brothers and sisters, the role of authority expressed by parents, loving concern for the members who are weaker because of youth, sickness, or old age, mutual help in the necessities of life, readiness to accept others and, if necessary, to forgive them.

---

[8] *Deus Caritas est* 11, §2.
[9] Cf. ibid. 44.
[10] *Africae munus* 43.

For this reason, the family is the first and indispensable teacher of peace."
By virtue of its central importance and the various threats looming over
it—distortion of the very notion of marriage and family, devaluation of
maternity and trivialization of abortion, easy divorce and the relativism of
a "new ethics"—the family needs to be protected and defended, so that
it may offer society the service expected of it, that of providing men and
women capable of building a social fabric of peace and harmony. (*Africae
munus* 43).

Pope Francis, highlighting the connection between family and
faith, writes in his first encyclical *Lumen fidei* (*The Light of Faith*), dated
June 29, 2013:

Encountering Christ, letting themselves be caught up in and guided by
his love, enlarges the horizons of existence, gives it a firm hope which
will not disappoint. Faith is no refuge for the fainthearted, but something
which enhances our lives. It makes us aware of a magnificent calling,
the vocation of love. It assures us that this love is trustworthy and worth
embracing, for it is based on God's faithfulness, which is stronger than
our every weakness.[11]

On *January 16, 2015*, during his meeting with Filipino families in
Manila, Pope Francis encouraged them to be "living examples of love,
forgiveness, and care. Be sanctuaries of respect for life, proclaiming
the sacredness of every human life from conception to natural death."
Before doing so, however, he remarked that "in the family we learn
how to love, to forgive, to be generous and open, not closed and selfish." At the end of the meeting, he addressed to them these words:
"When families bring children into the world, train them in faith and
sound values, and teach them to contribute to society, they become a
blessing in our world."[12]

3. Toward a New Culture of Human Life

   a. We have to face the bitter fact: "the family has become the object
      of multiple attacks." Because of this, we must arm ourselves

---

[11] *Lumen fidei* 53.
[12] Pope Francis, Address to the Meeting of Families, Manila, January 16, 2015.

appropriately to engage in and continue to the finish the noble battle to save the family at all costs. And at the heart of this already active threat that weighs heavily on the family are ongoing serious threats against human life.

b. Within the Holy Family that was just beginning, the Child Jesus was threatened with death by Herod from the very first days of his coming into the world in Bethlehem. And our Africa was a land of refuge, welcome, and hospitality for the Family of Jesus, Mary, and Joseph, which is given to us as a model for all our families. As Saint John Paul II perceived so well, Africa is the continent that must teach us by fresh efforts to rediscover and to respect scrupulously the meaning and the inestimable value of all human life, is it not?

> In African culture and tradition the role of the family is everywhere held to be fundamental. Open to this sense of the family, of love and respect for life, the African loves children, who are joyfully welcomed as gifts of God. "*The sons and daughters of Africa love life. . . .* The peoples of Africa respect the life which is conceived and born. They rejoice in this life. They reject the idea that it can be destroyed, even when the so-called 'progressive civilizations' would like to lead them in this direction. . . ." Africans show their respect for human life until its natural end and keep elderly parents and relatives within the family.[13]

c. Following the example of Saint John Paul II and Benedict XVI, not to forget Pope Francis, we all have the urgent duty to become champions of the splendor and absolute preeminence of LIFE over all the powers of death. We must set up a barrier against the "culture of death" by means of a genuine "mobilization for life". There has to be a vigorous response to the spreading "culture of death" by means of a "culture of life". Whether you are talking about conception, motherhood, birth, protection of the child, or respect for human life until its natural end, we are all called on to take up with courage and determination our mission of protecting, defending, and promoting human life, which is increasingly

---

[13] *Ecclesia in Africa* 43, §1, citing John Paul II, homily at the opening of the Special Assembly for Africa of the Synod of Bishops, April 10, 1994, paragraph 3.

being threatened. Saint John Paul II hammered this point home in *Evangelium vitae* as follows: "Everyone has an obligation to be at the service of life. This is a properly 'ecclesial' responsibility, which requires concerted and generous action by all the members and by all sectors of the Christian community" (EV 79, §3). As we know, being Christ's disciples, every human life, from the moment of conception until death, is sacred because the human person was willed for his or her own sake in the image and likeness of the living God, who is holy (see Gen 1:26). And "in order to fulfill its vocation as the 'sanctuary of life,' as the cell of a society which loves and welcomes life, *the family urgently needs to be helped and supported*.... For her part, the Church must untiringly promote a plan of pastoral care for families, capable of making every family rediscover and live with joy and courage its mission to further *the Gospel of life*."[14]

d. Finally, the Mother of all men and women who are reborn to life through Christ, the Virgin Mary is truly the Mother of Life who gives life to all men and all women. Therefore, we have valuable reasons to entrust to her the noble cause of life. By her intercession, may all who believe in her Son be able to proclaim firmly and lovingly, to the men and women of our times, the Gospel of life! May she obtain for us the grace to accept that Gospel as a gift that is ever new, the joy of celebrating it with thanksgiving throughout our lives, and the courage to witness to it actively and resolutely, so as to build up, with all people of goodwill, the civilization of truth and love, to the praise and glory of God the Creator who loves life (cf. *Evangelium vitae* 105)!

Conclusion

As the reader can tell even by perusing these few lines rather quickly, the recent Magisterium, since the Second Vatican Ecumenical Council, took to heart its duty to embark conscientiously on its important mission of informing, guiding, accompanying, and tirelessly encouraging the faithful to fulfill the demands of their vocation in matters concerning marriage and the family. It is appropriate to give thanks to the Lord of

---

[14] *Evangelium vitae* 94, §3 (emphasis added).

all goodness and benevolence for the good, beautiful, and admirable life that is being lived in a great number of homes and families.

The next ordinary synod of bishops, on the topic of "the Vocation and Mission of the Family in the Church and Contemporary World", will certainly not fail to enlighten us to perfection by appropriate doctrinal principles and pertinent, invaluable pastoral guidelines with a view to making pastoral care to the family as fruitful as possible. In no case can it be a matter of calling into question the fundamental truths about the sacrament of matrimony: unity, indissolubility, fidelity, and procreation, in other words, openness to new life.

Yes, more than ever, our era has a deep need of wisdom and expects that in one way or another the Church, as a good "Mother and Teacher", should lead to it. "Following Christ, the Church seeks the truth, which is not always the same as the majority opinion" (*Familiaris consortio* 5, §3). For this reason, while proving to be a merciful mother toward them and while sustaining them in faith and hope, as Saint John Paul II strongly recommended in his apostolic exhortation on "the role of the Christian family in the modern world", the Church, an "expert in humanity", has the urgent duty to reaffirm "her practice, which is based upon Sacred Scripture, of not admitting to Eucharistic Communion divorced persons who have remarried.... [I]f these people were admitted to the Eucharist, the faithful would be led into error and confusion regarding the Church's teaching about the indissolubility of marriage."[15] Finally, it is very important, in this connection, to make sure not to discourage or demoralize in any way "the young, who are beginning their journey towards marriage and family life", but rather address them "for the purpose of presenting them with new horizons, helping them to discover the beauty and grandeur of the vocation to love and the service of life".[16]

Yes, let us all work, each in his sphere, on this beauty and on this greatness of the vocation to love and to the service of life, for the future of our humanity passes through the family!

[15] *Familiaris consortio* 84, §4,
[16] Ibid. 1, §3.

The Indissolubility of Marriage

The Foundation of the Human Family

Philippe Cardinal Ouedraogo

Introduction

Our experience of the pastoral reality on African soil and especially in Burkina Faso as a priest and a bishop, through our effort to conduct a pastoral ministry of closeness or, to adopt the happy expressions of Pope Francis in *Evangelii gaudium*, pastoral practice that allows one to perceive "the smell of the sheep" (*EG* 24) or to reach life's peripheries (*EG* 20; 30), has lasted now for about forty years. Pastoral experience like this allows us to put our finger on the highlights and the dark spots of the family. Our pastoral observations were confirmed during the first Special Assembly for Africa of the Synod of Bishops, held in 1994. Indeed, the Synod Fathers pointed out many threats that weigh on the African family (*Ecclesia in Africa* 84). Nowadays, these threats remain present and even prove to have intensified within the context of secularization and globalization. They include divorce, gender ideology, the dictatorship of politically correct thinking, the ideological colonization of the family, insidiously orchestrated by international organizations whose aims are contrary to the values of the African and Christian family, and so on. It becomes necessary and urgent, then, to save the family through the promotion of values proposed by Scripture and Church teaching. Along these lines, the Word of God reveals to us the mystery of man and woman in the divine plan by telling us that the vocation to marriage is inscribed in the very nature of man and woman. So it is that God gradually unveiled the mystery of marriage through the weaving

Philippe Cardinal Ouedraogo is the metropolitan archbishop of Ouagadougou.

of the history of his people. Thus, the nuptial covenant between God and his people Israel, under the image of an exclusive, faithful conjugal love, had prepared the people's awareness for a deeper understanding of the unicity and indissolubility of marriage (Hos 1–3; Is 54; Ezek 16:23; Jer 2–3; 31; Mal 2:13–17). "In his preaching Jesus unequivocally taught the original meaning of the union of man and woman as the Creator willed it from the beginning.... The matrimonial union of man and woman is indissoluble: God himself has determined it: 'what therefore God has joined together, let no man put asunder'" (*Catechism of the Catholic Church* 1614, citing Mt 19:6).

In light of this teaching, the indissolubility of marriage appears to us to be an unshakable foundation on which the human family can be firmly built, in such a way as to promote human and Christian values better. Indissolubility is, in fact, one of the essential properties of marriage.[1] This essential quality of the union of man and woman appears from the moment of its institution at the beginning of creation: "Therefore a man leaves his father and his mother and clings to his wife, and they become one flesh" (Gen 2:24). It is subsequently repeated in the teaching of Christ[2] and the apostles.[3] This is because, faithful to this teaching, the tradition of the early Church in the first centuries categorically affirms the indissoluble character of the matrimonial bond, even in the case of adultery.

Most of the threats to which the family is exposed today are in one way or another connected with divorce, which in effect calls into question the indissolubility of marriage, the foundation and pledge of the human family. The theme of indissolubility to be discussed here will be addressed in three stages. First, we will note several challenges to indissolubility in a general way, and, second, in the case of mixed marriages and Islamo-Christian marriages in particular, we will see the challenges to indissolubility in the African cultural context. Finally, we will show that the Church's doctrine on the indissolubility of marriage allows us to meet all these challenges and, thereby, to shelter the human family definitively from all the insidious attacks to which it is increasingly subjected.

---

[1] Canon 1056 of the *Code of Canon Law* (1983): "The essential properties of marriage are unity and indissolubility, which in Christian marriage obtain a special firmness in virtue of the sacrament."

[2] Mt 19:1–8.

[3] Eph 5:31–32.

I. SOME CHALLENGES TO INDISSOLUBILITY IN OUR DAYS

In this first part of our essay, we wish to describe the phenomenon of the challenges to the indissolubility of marriage in our days in the African context. We are quite aware of the fact that this is a complex reality, but it is appropriate to sketch, even in broad strokes, these different challenges so as to be able to apply a consistent pastoral response. We will first address the challenges to indissolubility in a general way and, then, discuss challenges to indissolubility in the context of mixed and Islamo-Christian marriages.

A. In a General Way

We had occasion to emphasize in the introduction the importance of the influence of globalization, secularization, gender ideology, the dictatorship of one way of thinking, and the ideological colonization of the family in these times. An analysis of the reality of the challenges to indissolubility cannot help but pay attention to these facts. There is no need at all for us to go on in lengthy remarks, but it is clearly established that these different influences have an effect on human beings. Pope Benedict XVI, in *Africae munus*, following the Second Special Assembly for Africa of the Synod of Bishops, had pertinently diagnosed this problem by speaking about an anthropological crisis. Indeed, according to Benedict XVI,

> Men and women are shaped by their past, but they live and journey in the present, and they look ahead to the future. Like the rest of the world, Africa is experiencing a culture shock which strikes at the age-old foundations of social life and sometimes makes it hard to come to terms with modernity. In this anthropological crisis which the African continent is facing, paths of hope will be discovered by fostering dialogue among the members of its constituent religious, social, political, economic, cultural, and scientific communities. Africa will have to rediscover and promote a concept of the person and his or her relationship with reality that is the fruit of a profound spiritual renewal. (*AM* 11)

This anthropological crisis that affects African man causes him to live in a culture made up of things that are instantaneous, immediate, provisional, and fleeting. Only someone unfamiliar with the shock caused by this sort of culture could think that it does not affect sentiments and emotions, too. In this context, it is understandable that the model of marriage proposed by the Church is sometimes frightening because it is about committing oneself in the long term. Thus we are facing a crisis of long-term commitment. To speak about the indissolubility of marriage is to go against the current of the age, which advocates minimal effort, is reluctant to make sacrifices, and exalts love without fidelity. In these circumstances, one may wonder: How receptive are young people to the demands of marriage when they present themselves to ask to have their marriage celebrated in Church? In other words, is it necessary to ignore the fact that some young people are euphoric about their love story and go so far as to celebrate their marriage in the Church, heedless of the dimension of indissolubility in marriage? These are a few of the questions that challenge our pastoral ministry. In response to these serious questions, the diocesan synod of Ouagadougou issued guidelines that are still signposts for pastoral practice that enable us to meet these challenges. These guidelines include an effort to celebrate engagement in Christian base communities so that a commitment as important as the foundation of a Christian home might be made with the accompaniment and the blessing of the Christian family; attendance at obligatory marriage preparation courses; the establishment of one formation program for the whole archdiocese; and attention to Christian education for acquiring human, social, and Christian values. It is necessary to emphasize also the ongoing formation of our lay faithful at all levels and the regular follow-up of married couples. Finally, we must mention the guidelines of the "Pastoral Directory in the Church, the Family of God in Ouagadougou", which is a useful resource for pastoral practice along the lines of the new evangelization. This document enables pastors to assess the serious problems of pastoral practice and to find the appropriate pastoral approach in consultation. Yet although we have surveyed the challenges to the indissolubility of marriage in a general way, we must now analyze the cases of challenges to indissolubility in the context of mixed and Islamo-Christian marriages.

B. In the Context of Mixed and Islamo-Christian Marriages

In several real-life situations, the indissolubility of marriage is a real challenge for direct pastoral activity. This is the case with mixed marriages and, generally speaking, with marriages involving disparity of cult, more particularly Islamo-Christian marriages.

1. Mixed marriages and indissolubility

Marriage between two baptized persons is a sacramental marriage that acquires its full sacramental character in a ratified, consummated marriage. In preparing for marriage, and according to the requirements to be fulfilled in order that the local Ordinary may authorize a mixed marriage, canon law stipulates that "Both parties are to be instructed on the essential ends and properties of marriage, which are not to be excluded by either party" (can. 1125, §3). Now for some Protestant denominations, marriage is not a sacrament. Nor is there a celebration of marriage as such, but rather a prayer blessing the matrimonial bond that is sealed in the presence of an official of the civil state, for example. It follows that the civil authority does not consider civil marriage to be indissoluble.

Although the Catholic party, in contracting marriage, commits himself in a sacramental marriage whose indissolubility has particular stability, the same cannot be said of the non-Catholic baptized party. Hence this is a serious handicap, inasmuch as the fact that the two spouses are baptized automatically makes their union sacramental: "For this reason a matrimonial contract cannot validly exist between baptized persons unless it is also a sacrament by that fact" (can. 1055, §2). Should mixed marriages therefore be forbidden, in the name of the indissolubility of the matrimonial bond, the importance of which is not necessarily perceived by the non-Catholic party, who, consequently, does not feel morally and spiritually obliged to respect it? We want to avoid the pitfall denounced by Pope Francis when he said that as pastors we often behave like arbiters of grace and not as facilitators (EG 47); even so, it must be acknowledged that experience suggests greater pastoral prudence in precisely these cases. Thus our diocesan synod, noting the significant percentage of failures recorded, particularly in mixed marriages, recommended that the parents and pastors of young people stress the major difficulties of mixed marriage.

As for the young people, they must have greater respect for their Catholic faith and not run the risk of compromising it. Certainly, we believe in the primacy of grace, but our pastoral care is offered as a mission to help young people to see clearly the great delicacy of the question.

2. Islamo-Christian marriages and indissolubility

The problem just mentioned with some mixed marriages is relevant in marriages where there is disparity of cult, and in Islamo-Christian marriages in particular. Indeed, in Muslim marriage, repudiation is the husband's right. Thus, in a disparate, Islamo-Christian marriage, even though the Muslim party is asked not to exclude the ends and the essential properties of marriage, obviously several days of simple instruction or even a written engagement would not be enough to elicit firm adherence to the principle of the indissolubility of marriage. Hence, how can two such divergent concepts be reconciled in such an important institution? Just as in the case of mixed marriage, our diocesan synod also noted a significant percentage of failures in marriages with disparity of cult. Besides the pastoral care already recommended for mixed marriages—care that applies also to the present cases—our diocesan synod recommended taking additional measures to safeguard the faith of young Catholic believers. These measures are to be specified on a case-to-case basis depending on the particular situations. Indeed, every situation needs to be viewed with pastoral mercy but also in the light of truth.

The question becomes even more acute when the couple is on the verge of breaking up. For then the Muslim party, although aware of the indissolubility of Christian marriage, tends to take advantage of the situation by purely and simply denying any indissolubility, since there is no such thing in Islam or in civil law. This state of mind, as anyone can see, is a weakness inherent in mixed marriages generally and in disparate marriage in particular. Hence the pertinence of the question: Should mixed and disparate marriages not be forbidden so as to safeguard the indissolubility of marriage? Such a measure may seem excessive, but is a life of faith conceivable without the cross? Indeed, for the sake of the faith and of his life with Christ, the believer must be able to make the choice that involves the acceptance of the cross and the renunciation of his own plans. But a person can accept all these sacrifices only when a Christian education truly enables him to live as an adult and to make consistent choices. This is the objective that our diocesan pastoral plan aims to accomplish.

II. CHALLENGES TO THE INDISSOLUBILITY OF THE MATRIMONIAL BOND IN THE AFRICAN CULTURAL CONTEXT

A. Indissolubility Put to the Test by Sterility and Procreation

In several African cultures, marriage is not only an alliance between a man and a woman, but also and above all *an alliance between two families*. In former times, the two families were the ones who arranged everything, even against the will of the young woman or of the young man. In our days, more and more, the young woman and the young man choose each other freely but turn to representatives of the two families to make the official, public announcement of their future union.

Thus there is an alliance between the young woman's family and the young man's; this means that the matrimonial bond is not subject to the whims of the spouses. In effect the two families assume the duty of vigilance to maintain the matrimonial bond on which their honor depends. From this perspective, the groom's family has much more responsibility, so much so that his conduct is supervised much more by his relatives. In this matter, the honor of each party must be intact, so as to be a pledge of trust between the two families and to allow still other alliances.

The two families act in such a way as to guarantee this common good, the principal elements of which are the alliance and procreation. The alliance based on their given word calls for a mutual commitment of each party with strict observance of the terms. Such dispositions in alliances are a pledge of stability, even sometimes in such a delicate situation as that of an *infertile couple*. Infertility is one of the most delicate marital problems in most African cultures. Indeed, procreation is so important in marriage that for some people it is the principal objective of the marital union, which, viewed from the social perspective, is not only a means of cohesion through the interplay of alliances, but also a means of increasing and perpetuating one's posterity. Hence, a certain stability of the conjugal bond must be guaranteed for the good of the spouses and especially of the children, who need a harmonious setting in which to grow and flourish. Children are a good for the whole family, because they will make it survive. This concept of marriage and of the family in no way depends on the spouses alone.

Furthermore, with regard to the generation of children, in some clans or ethnic groups procreation is viewed on the spiritual level as a gift from God, so that no one can be blamed for sterility. Therefore, in many cultures in Africa, *sterility* does not affect the indissolubility of the marital bond. The husband is bound to keep and to care for his sterile wife, even though he is allowed to take a second wife so as to ensure the permanence of the family. But then, in authorizing polygamy in order to remedy the problem of sterility, are they not by that very fact denying the indissolubility of marriage? Certainly! But pastoral care for the family cannot ignore this cultural and sociological fact, which is a challenge that must be met through an inculturation of the faith—inculturation understood here as the Fathers of the Church do, as a "transforming conversion".[4] In the light of Christ, the believer becomes aware of the values of his culture but also of its deficiencies, which are the mark of sin and call for conversion.

B. Indissolubility Put to the Test by Some Cultural Circumstances in Daily Life

The marital alliance between the husband and the wife, which has repercussions on the two families, is based on their given word and may be revocable by way of exception in precise and very limited circumstances. Since the alliance is a mutual commitment between the parties, they are bound to respect absolutely the terms of the pact. It sometimes happens, though, that certain sorts of behavior seriously endanger the pact, the alliance, and the conjugal bond and, thereby, the indissolubility of marriage.

Thus for example, in several princely families among the Moose [Mossi] in Burkina Faso, once the marriage is consummated, the wife's adultery with another member of her husband's family is punished irrevocably by the dissolution of the marital bond. Consequently, the wife is dismissed, and her accomplice is banished from the family. In contrast, the children remain part of the family. In the case of a married man who commits the same crime with a woman of the family, he is banished.

There are also seemingly trivial gestures that, if made by one or the other spouse, are a threat to the stability of the home. Some gestures—such as a wife biting her husband—can lead to a break-up of the marital bond. Others—such as the husband scattering the stones that make up

---

[4] We refer the reader in this connection to the major conference given by Joseph Cardinal Ratzinger in Hong Kong in 1993 on "Inculturation or Interculturality?"

the fireplace for cooking—are an act of repudiating the wife. This act occurs generally after a series of offenses committed by the wife. Even though in both cases acts of reparation are possible, nevertheless these customs challenge the indissolubility of marriage. Hence what attitude is appropriate to adopt in similar situations, in order to avoid being in an awkward position with one's Christian faith and with the surrounding culture? This situation helps us to understand how urgent it is for us to work, once again, for the inculturation of the faith. Without this inculturation, which takes into account the richness of the culture and makes possible the purification thereof, our Church will have difficulty facilitating a welcome of Jesus Christ into the African way of life as a whole. Thus we understand even better all that is at stake in the question of inculturation in our day.

C. The Indissolubility of Marriage Put to the Test by Some Activities by Officials

Within the framework of this reflection on the indissolubility of marriage, we could also mention several situations that require more than one pastoral solution. We are talking essentially about problems that appear in the context of the activities of Church officials. In fact, not uncommonly, non-baptized persons, with a view of contracting marriage with a Catholic party, come to them asking for baptism. Depending on the case, the baptism is administered before or after the marriage. But if the marriage happens to break up, the convert immediately returns to his religion of origin.

Even though there is no rule that conversion is a condition for mixed or disparate marriage, one may wonder whether this is not the idea in the minds of the interested parties. Apart from the fact that a judicial or extra-judicial investigation may reveal a specific canonical cause of nullity, such situations, while adding to the fragility of the indissolubility of marriage, pose the problem of the status of each of the separated spouses, but especially of the previously baptized party. For the one who left the faith, is it not necessary to call into question his sincerity with regard to his request for baptism? What happens to the bond in this case? In these cases we are dealing with human situations that are sometimes tragic. But the Church is a father's house in which there is room for everyone with his difficult life (EG 47). And so, at the end of long investigations, it will be possible to make a balanced judgment and, depending on the situation, to propose an attempted solution to a complicated situation.

Another situation, which is confusing in the view of the persons concerned, is that of two non-baptized persons who have contracted a customary or civil marriage and then receive baptism, each in turn or both together. It is always the case that their marriage has become sacramental and is now under the seal of intrinsic indissolubility. But in the minds of the interested parties, since they did not contract their union in the form of the ordinary celebration with the exchange of their consent, they tell themselves that they are not married in the Church. For them it is unthinkable to mention any sort of indissolubility of their union, if they do not go so far as to exclude it outright. They become even more set in this way of thinking if nothing was done by way of a paraliturgy including the exchange of wedding rings and the nuptial blessing of the spouses. Does this situation not pose once again the question about the indissolubility of marriage? Indeed, these situations remind us of the need for an in-depth catechesis that enables Christians to know their faith better. But the appropriate pastoral attitude consists of indicating the sacramental dimension of marriage and of its indissoluble character through the blessing and the exchange of wedding rings.

In Church doctrine, indissolubility concerns every marriage. However, another situation leads us to pose the problem of indissolubility in the case of a marriage celebrated in the Church with a dispensation for disparity of cult and also before a civil official. In the event of civil divorce, since the Church does not recognize it, the couple remain bound. This situation is of concern to both of them. The Catholic party could possibly benefit from a request to dissolve their marriage. As for the non-baptized party, if, before a possible dissolution of the bond, he or she expresses the desire to be married with another Catholic party, there will be reason to prevent this new marriage by not granting the dispensation for that future spouse. But if, on the other hand, the non-baptized party remarried with a non-Catholic party, it would be difficult in practice to subject him to the consequences of the situation that he shares with the Catholic party by reason of their previous marriage, inasmuch as the non-baptized party feels that the Church's discipline is not his concern and that, besides, the Church has no ability to constrain him in any way. The indissolubility of marriage again would be challenged.

All things considered, one might, at the end of the multiple trials to which it has been subjected, rightly wonder whether they do not begin to weaken the deeply protective character of the indissolubility of marriage. Hence the need to set forth clearly the doctrine of the Church concerning the indissolubility of the marital bond, in such a way that the various challenges mentioned above not only do not trouble the faith of Christians in the indissolubility of marriage, but most importantly are met and resolved through it.

III. THE INDISSOLUBILITY OF MARRIAGE ACCORDING TO CHURCH TEACHING

Given the different pastoral situations described above, some of which are not unique to the contemporary era, inasmuch as they already appeared in the ancient and/or recent history of the Church, we understand that the interpretation of the passages relating to the principle of indissolubility has not always been easy. Nevertheless, it must be admitted that the difficulties and doubts have not prevented a strong affirmation of the absolute indissolubility of marriage.

Although the Council of Trent, faithful to the traditional doctrine of the Church, affirms the Church's authority with regard to the indissolubility of the marital bond (cf. DS 1807), she has nevertheless not defined it solemnly. This has not prevented her from continuing to teach that a validly established conjugal bond can neither be dissolved nor excluded by the will of the spouses.

Nonetheless, particular situations encountered by some couples may have affected the manner in which this principle is applied, without however calling it into question. It is also well established that even adultery, despite the interpretations of some authors and Fathers of the Church, cannot dissolve marriage: "But if the Church has not erred and does not err when she has taught or teaches this, and it is therefore completely certain that marriage cannot be dissolved even for the cause of adultery, it is clear that other weaker reasons for divorce that are usually presented count for even less and must be considered as completely baseless."[5] Faithful to Church tradition, the 1983 Code of Canon Law

---

[5] Cf. DH 1807.

exhorts the injured spouse to forgive in the case of adultery, except when that proves to be impossible. In that case the separation of the spouses can occur, while maintaining, however, the marital bond.[6] This official position of the Church is even more clear-cut with regard to sacramental marriage. Indeed, although indissolubility, like unity, is true of every marriage, it acquires particular solidity in Christian marriage, by reason of the sacrament.[7] "The essential properties of marriage are unity and indissolubility, which in Christian marriage obtain a special firmness in virtue of the sacrament" (can. 1056).

As emphasized above, in some eras, in the Church, there was not always a unanimous opinion about the indissolubility of marriage in the case of adultery. The Council did not fail to point out this hesitation, which results mainly from the interpretation of the interpolation in Matthew 19:9, "except for unchastity" ("And I say to you: whoever divorces his wife, *except for unchastity*, and marries another, commits adultery").[8] Indeed, despite these differences, the Church has always defended the indissolubility of marriage, especially because further reflection has led her to distinguish habitually between intrinsic indissolubility and extrinsic indissolubility.

---

[6] Canon 1152, §1: "Although it is earnestly recommended that a spouse, moved by Christian charity and a concern for the good of the family, not refuse pardon to an adulterous partner and not break up conjugal life, nevertheless, if the spouse has not expressly or tacitly condoned the misdeed of the other spouse, the former does have the right to sever conjugal living, unless he or she consented to the adultery, gave cause for it, or likewise committed adultery."

§2: "Tacit condonation exists if the innocent spouse, after having become aware of the adultery, continued voluntarily to live with the other spouse in marital affection. Tacit condonation is presumed if the innocent spouse continued conjugal living for a period of six months and has not had recourse to ecclesiastical or civil authority."

§3: "If the innocent spouse spontaneously severed conjugal living, that spouse within six months is to bring a suit for separation before the competent ecclesiastical authority; this authority, after having investigated all the circumstances, is to decide whether the innocent spouse can be induced to forgive the misdeed and not to prolong the separation permanently."

[7] Canon 1055, §1: "The matrimonial covenant, by which a man and a woman establish between themselves a partnership of the whole of life, is by its nature ordered toward the good of the spouses and the procreation and education of offspring; this covenant between baptized persons has been raised by Christ the Lord to the dignity of a sacrament."

[8] In the Ecumenical Translation of the Bible [*Traduction oecuménique de la Bible; la Bible TOB*], a note at Matthew 5:32 says: "Here and at 19:9 the word translated [in French] as 'illicit union' is interpreted in three main senses: 1. Something shameful (see Deut 24:1).... 2. Adultery, i.e., the wife's infidelity to her husband.... 3. Illegal conjugal union, especially according to the legislation in Lev 18:6–18...."

A. Intrinsic Indissolubility

Indissolubility means that a validly established matrimonial bond is perpetual. Such a marriage cannot be subject to a divorce for any reason whatsoever. The intrinsic indissolubility of marriage is considered under three aspects:

1. From the spouses' perspective

Since it is a loving union involving the total and perpetual mutual gift of the man and the woman, marriage is an indissoluble unity of the spouses. The intimate union that constitutes marriage and engages the whole person of the spouses can only be indissoluble. The spouses must seek to save it by all means in case of difficulty. The indissolubility of marriage is not an element external or incidental to conjugal love. It is a property of authentic love that is the gift of self. Authentic love is definitive, not temporary. This is why the union that it generates is indissoluble. Hence the moral obligation for the spouses to protect and preserve their conjugal covenant in an unfailing mutual love, for their own good (*bonum connubii*) and for the good of their children (*bonum prolis*).

If it is true that indissolubility is a property of authentic love that is the gift of self, is it possible to conceive of a matrimonial bond or a conjugal covenant that is not at the same time marked with the seal of indissolubility? In other words, without the principle of indissolubility, can we really speak about marriage? Does the institution of marriage have any reality or substance apart from indissolubility? Every marriage presupposes by the very fact the principle and the ideal of indissolubility, for which Christ's unfailing fidelity to his Church is the paradigm and model.

2. From God's perspective

The human act performed by the spouses in mutually giving and receiving one another is willed by God. For this reason, the matrimonial bond is not subject to the will of man and to the free choice of the spouses. The indissolubility of marriage is truly founded on the bond itself according to the divine will that is inscribed in creation: "A man ... clings to his wife, and they become one flesh" (Gen 2:24), and in keeping with the requirements willed by God from the beginning and recalled by Christ:

"What therefore God has joined together, let no man put asunder" (Mt 19:6). Indeed, it cannot be repeated enough that "conjugal union is not merely a human institution but a work of God. This grace-filled event confers on marriage a sacred character that situates it beyond what the spouses can control."[9] As the Council declares: "The sacred bond no longer depends on human decisions alone."[10] Hence one could not be a genuinely Catholic Christian and try to sacrifice the indissolubility of marriage in the name of certain cultural values.

3. In relation to Christ

Considered from the Christological perspective, the indissolubility of Christian marriage has its foundation in Christ's relationship with his Church. Indeed, Christian marriage "is the image, sacrament, and witness of the indissoluble union between Christ and the Church".[11] This constitutes "the good of the sacrament".

> Of all the properties of marriage, indissolubility is the one that most clearly signifies its sacramental aspect (bonum sacramenti). In the Christian tradition, the symbolism of the union of Christ and his Church is the foundation of the indissolubility of Christian marriage. God's favors are unconditional and irrevocable. The "yes" of Christian spouses participates in the permanent "yes" of God to man in Christ: the spouses receive the grace and the power to be faithful as God himself is. Christ's "yes" to the spouses is expressed through their own "yes". In giving themselves to one another, they are given by Christ, who makes himself the guarantor responsible for their mutual gift and, at the price of his blood, gives them the strength to love each other to the end.[12]

Because of the fact that Christ becomes the guarantor responsible for the mutual gift of Christian spouses in particular, but of all spouses in general—even unbeknownst to them—it is impossible to separate indissolubility from any marital institution, from any conjugal covenant.

---

[9] Édouard Hamel, "Indissolubilité", in Commission Théologique International (CTI), *Problèmes doctrinaux du mariage chrétien* (Louvain-la-Neuve, distributed by Centre Cerfaux-Lefort, 1979), 109.

[10] GS 48.1.

[11] Hamel, "Indissolubilité", 108.

[12] Ibid., 110.

4. From the social perspective

In this regard, indissolubility is at the service of the institution itself. The personal commitment of the spouses is ratified, protected, and strengthened by society, especially by the Christian community. In this sense, the indissolubility of marriage is a common good for society as a whole, just as it benefits children. This is why it must always be safeguarded, for to sell it off is to destroy the human family at its root, to deprive it of its foundation. We can understand, then, the resulting estrangement of the human family, after the thoughtlessness with which the marital bond is broken today, with a complete lack of concern and absolute casualness toward the ideal of the indissolubility of marriage. Hence, in order to save the decaying human family, it would be necessary to begin by granting to the principle and ideal of the indissolubility of marriage its full importance and the place that belongs to it in the Church and in society.

These various aspects that have just been mentioned are closely interconnected, so much so that the fidelity required of spouses should be under the protection of society as a whole and at the ecclesial level.

B. Extrinsic Indissolubility and the Church's Authority over Marriages

The Church has always considered that Christ's words, "what God has joined together, let no man put asunder", remove the conjugal bond from the decision and whims of the spouses. Nevertheless, on the subject of marriage, she has developed a doctrine defining the boundaries of her own authority over the matrimonial bond. Thus, the Church claims no authority to dissolve a sacramental marriage that has been ratified and consummated (*ratum et consummatum*).[13] However, "for very serious reasons, for the good of the faith and the salvation of souls, other marriages can be dissolved by the competent authority or, according to one interpretation, can be declared dissolved in and of themselves."[14] The possibility of dissolving some marriages for the sake of the faith is due to the fact that the firmness of the bond varies depending on the case, for instance, the marriage between a baptized person and another who is not baptized.

[13] Code of Canon Law (1983), can. 1118.
[14] Hamel, "Indissolubilité", 113.

From this perspective, it should be remembered that what is considered by some to be a power of the Church to dissolve a marriage is regarded by others as "a simple power of declaration". Thus the Church would do nothing but observe and declare the non-existence of a bond. And in the case of the Pauline privilege, for example, the marriage of the party benefiting from the privilege would annul the first bond with the party who wished to separate, and not some authority of the diocesan bishop or of the Supreme Pontiff in other cases. Moreover, the fact that the Church does not claim to have the power to dissolve a ratified and consummated marriage is also explained in different ways. Whereas some think that she voluntarily ruled out that authority, others deny it outright. This is the case with Pius XII: "The bond of Christian marriage is so strong that if it has attained its full permanence with the use of conjugal rights, no power on earth, not even Ours, the power of the Vicar of Christ, can rescind it."[15] The Church's declaration that she is not competent to dissolve a ratified and consummated marriage is said to be explained by the fact that " 'the mystical signification of Christian marriage ... is fully and perfectly verified in consummated marriage between Christians. For, as the apostle says in his Epistle to the Ephesians, the marriage of Christians recalls that most perfect union that exists between Christ and the Church (Eph 5:32).' Since the mystery of Christ's union with the Church is perfectly signified only in a consummated sacramental union, only in this case does the indissolubility of marriage become absolute and not come under the Church's authority. A non-consummated sacramental union remains incomplete."[16]

What, then, would be the exact role of carnal consummation in marriage? What would it add to the sacramentality of the bond, since according to the Code of Canon Law: "The marriage covenant ... between baptized persons has been raised by Christ the Lord to the dignity of a sacrament", and "for this reason a matrimonial contract cannot validly exist between baptized persons unless it is also a sacrament by that fact"?[17] The answer is that:

In consummating their loving union, Christian spouses truly become one flesh. Their covenant is perfect and then fully represents the indissoluble

[15]Pius XII, Address, March 16, 1946; cited in ibid., 115.
[16]Hamel, "Indissolubilité", 115, citing Pius XI, *Casti Connubii*, 36.
[17]See can. 1055.

union between Christ and his Church. The consummation therefore does not add to the sacramental character: it is part of it, it gives it its fullness. A ratified and consummated marriage is, indeed, a fully sacramental marriage. This is why it is absolutely indissoluble.[18]

C. The Challenge of Inculturation, or African Culture in the Service of Indissolubility

Inculturation is always a challenge that must be met. History teaches us that we must take into account the genius of a culture in order to calibrate the message of salvation in such a way that every nation may proclaim Christ with its values. In this regard, Pope Francis' reminder is an encouragement to continue along the path of inculturation that can never end. The pope correctly teaches us that "We would not do justice to the logic of the incarnation if we thought of Christianity as monocultural and monotonous. While it is true that some cultures have been closely associated with the preaching of the Gospel and the development of Christian thought, the revealed message is not identified with any of them; its content is transcultural" (*EG* 117). By dint of this statement by Pope Francis, we can say that the second part of our argument allowed us to bring to light some values of African culture that are like ramparts and guard rails in the defense of the indissolubility of Christian marriage. This acknowledgment is not an indiscriminate canonization of all African cultural values, but rather an instance of "seeing reality with the eyes of faith, [whereby] we cannot fail to acknowledge what the Holy Spirit is sowing" (*EG* 68). Among the values sowed by the Holy Spirit we can recognize: the matrimonial bond, which is not subject to the whims of the spouses and also involves their families, marriage as an alliance between two families, the weight of the word that is given, the fact that sterility does not affect the indissolubility of the bond, acts of reparation with a view to reconciliation, and so on. A pastoral plan that aims to strengthen the foundation of the family cannot do without these sociological and cultural facts that can be brought out so as to help African Christian spouses to persevere in their total mutual gift of themselves in faithfulness to the promise pronounced on their wedding day. We are well aware that the pastoral plan of inculturating these elements of the culture needs to be examined in greater depth so as not to be a thin coat of varnish that is not weather resistant.

---

[18] Hamel, "Indissolubilité", 116.

D. Indissolubility and Remarriage

In connection with the social aspect of intrinsic indissolubility, it seems to us important to touch on the phenomenon of the remarriage of divorced persons, even though it is expected that another essay will address this at greater length and in more depth.

Remarriage after divorce will always be a disvalue from the social perspective, for it inevitably tends to undermine the stability of marriage by reducing the likelihood of resuming common life in homes that, although in crisis, are still capable of being rebuilt after a new surge of fidelity by the spouses.

The prohibitions against the remarriage of spouses is not based solely on the indissolubility of their own union, but also, and perhaps more so, on the indissolubility of other people's marriages.

It is important to tell the spouses that indissolubility is not simply an arrangement of the Church. Moreover, even in the case where marriage between Christians comes partly from the will of the spouses, it is determined even more by the will of Christ. Indeed,

> the personal commitment of the spouses is made at the very heart of the sacrament that is given and received: Christ's covenantal will is incarnated in the indissoluble sacramental bond that unites the spouses. The indissolubility of marriage between Christians is not based therefore on their personal commitment alone; it must be considered a profound, mysterious reality, a manifestation of the very mystery of God. However, this sacramental *vinculum* [bond]—marriage, sign of Christ's covenant with his Church—is translated in turn into a moral obligation to fidelity. By Christ's will, the spouses are ordained to one another, in a permanent, reciprocal obligation to pursue dialogue, forgiveness, and reconciliation.[19]

Indissolubility partakes of the constant fidelity of the spouses. Indeed, what maintains the stability of the marital partnership is not so much the legal contract itself as the mutual commitment of the spouses to be faithful to one another. Ultimately, their fidelity is rooted in the grace of Christ that is at work at the very heart of their personal commitment. Even though grace does not create indissolubility, it perfects it.

[19] Ibid., 112.

Conclusion

By way of conclusion, it is appropriate to emphasize, following Pope Saint John Paul II, that "the future of the world and of the Church passes through the family",[20] for it is the primordial cell of the living ecclesial community, but also of society. In Africa in particular, the family is a fundamental institution in social and ecclesial life. So it is not right to allow the Christian, African family to be trampled on and destroyed. In the midst of the challenges and threats that weigh upon the family today, an urgent appeal ought to resound in the hearts of everyone, inciting them to conversion and commitment to the service of the Gospel of the Family, through respect for the indissolubility of marriage that is its unshakable foundation.

In this perspective, the evangelical ideal of the indissolubility of marriage is an unprecedented grace destined to save the human family from any decline. To Christian families that, despite the obstacles, do their best to live out this ideal, we express our admiration and gratitude for this witness of faith rendered to Christ in love and fidelity. May their example motivate those persons who, in their marital life, are going through trials or are still laboring along the path of authentic Christian witness and wrongly suppose that by abandoning the ideal of the indissolubility of marriage they will be fulfilled and find true happiness.

For our African pastors, experience proves that it is necessary and salutary to bring fully to light, not contingent philosophical, anthropological, or cultural views, but above all the patrimony of faith that the Church has the duty to preserve in its inviolable purity, in other words, the ideal of marital and familial life proposed by biblical revelation and manifested essentially by the indissolubility of marriage. Furthermore, it is urgent to present this ideal to the men and women of our time in a comprehensible and persuasive way, while offering light, meaning, and hope to all.

We thank God for having inspired our Holy Father Francis to convoke a general assembly of the synod of bishops on the topic of marriage and the family (October 2014 and October 2015). May these pastors and the Christian communities always take care to accompany the internal rifts and social strains of couples and families and to commend them to

---

[20] John Paul II, *Familiaris consortio* (1981), 75.

the Divine Mercy. After the example of the Holy Family of Nazareth—"prototype and example for all Christian families"[21]—may our families accomplish fully their mission to be authentic "domestic churches", "intimate partnership(s) of life and love",[22] in the image of the Church, for the indissolubility of her wedding with Christ is the pledge and paradigm for the indissolubility of marriage that is the basis of our human families in general and of our Christian families in particular.

To all of them, may the help of divine grace always be offered, without which human efforts and battles are doomed to failure and despair. With his grace and through his Word of life, Christ consoles, heals, saves, and always calls us to hope. Following her Master, "The Church is called to be the house of the Father, with doors always wide open.... It is the house of the Father, where there is a place for everyone, with all their problems" (EG 47).

So it should be also with our human families that, in the midst of different challenges to the indissolubility of marriage, must never lose sight of the fact that they are nevertheless domestic churches, in which Christ is always present, so that his unfailing fidelity to his Church may triumph over our multiple marital infidelities, transforming them into paths of salvation for human families.

[21] See Ecclesia in Africa 81.
[22] GS 48.

Promoting a True Understanding of Marriage and the Accompaniment of Married Couples

Berhaneyesus D. Cardinal Souraphiel, C.M.

Abstract

Marriage is based on the truth that men and women are complementary, the biological fact that reproduction depends on a man and a woman, and the reality that children need a mother and a father. Marriage is society's least restrictive means of ensuring the well-being of children. By encouraging the norms of marriage—monogamy, sexual exclusivity, and permanence—the state strengthens civil society and reduces its own role. The future of marriage depends on citizens understanding what it is and why it matters and demanding that government policies support, not undermine, true marriage.

Human beings need relationships because they are made in God's image. A man by himself is not complete; neither is a woman. They each need a soul mate. A man needs a woman as his helper and mate and vice-versa (Gen 2:18). We need a range of relationships. The marriage relationship is the most intimate human relationship, based on covenant and faithfulness. Any relationship by itself does not make a true relationship. True completeness comes through union with Christ (Col 2:10), and that applies to everyone, children, single persons, and married persons alike.

Unity is another part of God's personality—the Father, the Son, and the Holy Spirit are one. Such unity is reflected in creation, particularly, with human beings, in sacramental marriage. We can find the closest relationship between a man and a woman in the Bible, where this relationship is called to be "one flesh".

Marriage exists to bring a man and a woman together as husband and wife and as father and mother to any children their sexual union

Berhaneyesus D. Cardinal Souraphiel, C.M., is metropolitan archbishop of Addis Abeba, president of the CBCE, and chairman of AMECEA.

produces. It is based on the anthropological truth that men and women are different and complementary, the biological fact that reproduction depends on a man and a woman, and the social reality that children need both a mother and a father. The question is whether a father will be involved in the life of those children and, if so, for how long. Marriage increases the odds that a man will be committed both to the children he helps create and to the woman with whom he does so. Marriage predates government. Marriage has public purposes that transcend its private purposes.

The "great mystery" of spousal love, the spousal love of Christ and his Bride the Church and the spousal love of husband and wife joined together by our Triune God, manifest to the world that God is relationship oriented. In conjugal intimacy, the reality and dignity of both spouses are founded on divine fatherhood. The roles of fathers and mothers are complementary and inseparable; they both presume the creation of specific, interpersonal relationships between the parents and the children. Every child has a right to be born of a father and a mother joined in conjugal love.

Because of this great mystery of love and life that flows from the marriage bond, the family is "the first and vital cell of society" (*Apostolicam actuositatem* 11) and of the Church. Where marriages flourish in virtue, the Church prospers with life, and society becomes a civilization of love.

What is marriage?

Marriage is the union of a man and woman who make a permanent and exclusive commitment to each other of the type that is naturally (inherently) fulfilled by bearing and rearing children together. The spouses seal (consummate) and renew their union by conjugal acts—acts that constitute the behavioral part of the process of reproduction, thus uniting them as a reproductive unit. Marriage is valuable in itself, but its inherent orientation to the bearing and rearing of children contributes to its distinctive structure, including norms of monogamy and fidelity. This link to the welfare of children also helps explain why marriage is important to the common good and why the state should recognize and regulate it. As such, marriage is the type of social practice whose basic forms can be discerned by our common human reason, whatever our religious background. "Men and women of full age, without any limitation due to race, nationality or religion, have the right to marry and to found a family. They are entitled to equal rights as to marriage, during marriage and at its dissolution" (*Universal Declaration of Human Rights*, art. 16).

Marriage is more than a physical relationship. It is a spiritual relationship as well. "The right to each other's body" must not be understood in a materialistic way. Sexuality cannot be isolated from the whole of married life and from the countless attentions that married love requires. The right to the marriage act constitutes an essential element of the marriage covenant. The refusal of marital submission for a considerable time without a just motive is the violation of marital love.

Almost every culture in every time and place has had some institution that resembles what we know as marriage. Marriage is the kind of union that is shaped by its comprehensiveness and fulfilled by procreation and child-rearing. Only this can account for its essential features, which make less sense in other relationships. Because marriage uniquely meets essential needs in such a structured way, it should be regulated for the common good, which can be understood apart from specifically religious arguments. Marriage understood as the conjugal union of husband and wife really serves the good of children, the good of spouses, and the common good of society.

Marriage as the union of man and woman is true across cultures, religions, and time. The government recognizes but does not create marriage. Marriage is the fundamental building block of all human civilization. The government does not create marriage. Marriage is a natural institution that predates government. Society as a whole, not merely any given set of spouses, benefits from marriage. This is because marriage helps to channel procreative love into a stable institution that provides for the orderly bearing and rearing of the next generation. Marriage also gives rise to an entirely original community, formed by a man and a woman, which affects the present and the future of society and the Church.

This understanding of marriage as the union of man and woman is shared by the Jewish, Christian, and Muslim traditions; by ancient Greek and Roman thinkers untouched by these religions; and by various Enlightenment philosophers. It is affirmed by both common and civil law and by ancient Greek and Roman law.

As with other public policy issues, religious voices on marriage should be welcomed in the public square. Yet one need not appeal to distinctively religious arguments to understand why marriage—as a natural institution—is the union of man and woman.

Key points

1. Marriage exists to bring a man and a woman together as husband and wife to be father and mother to any children their union produces.
2. Marriage is based on the truth that men and women are complementary, the biological fact that reproduction depends on a man and a woman, and the reality that children need both a mother and a father.
3. Marriage is society's least restrictive means of ensuring the well-being of children. The breakdown of marriage weakens the civil society and endangers limited government, as the state takes over the functions proper to the family.
4. Government recognizes marriage because it benefits society in a way that no other relationship does.
5. Government can treat people equally and respect their liberty without redefining marriage.
6. Redefining marriage would further distance marriage from the needs of children and deny the importance of mothers and fathers; weaken monogamy, exclusivity, and permanency, the norms through which marriage benefits society; and threaten religious liberty.

The family is a school of love

A stable family is the building block of society that allows persons to flourish as human beings. Families are centers of living and radiant faith where discipleship is lived out and where religious vocations are fostered (*CCC* 1656, 2232–33). The *Catechism of the Catholic Church* tells us that "the home is the first school of Christian life" and "a school for human enrichment" where "one learns endurance and the joy of work, fraternal love, generous—even repeated—forgiveness, and above all divine worship in prayer and the offering of one's life" (*CCC* 1657). Pope Emeritus Benedict XVI, during his visit to the United States, took several opportunities to encourage families in their common vocation and to exhort all other members of society to work for the strengthening of marriages and family life.

Pope Emeritus Benedict XVI points out in his encyclical *Spe salvi* that the news of hope in Christ proclaimed by the Gospel is not a piece of information to be stowed away in one's subconscious. Because of faith in Christ, our everyday lives should be continuously transformed and conformed to Christ as we encounter God, transforming and conforming society to Christ along the way. The transformation that parents choose to undergo and nurture in their children is especially important as they try to (1) foster opportunities for conversion in their families and work to bring the encounter with God to maturity, (2) encourage their children to grow in deeper knowledge and love of God, and (3) help them establish a firm commitment to living the faith.

"Marriage and the family are ordered to the good of the spouses and to the procreation and education of children. The love of the spouses and the begetting of children create among members of the same family personal relationships and primordial responsibilities" (*CCC* 2201).

Living in the future now

The meaning of our lives is not an experience or a fullness of life attainable only in the future. As Christians full of hope, "Faith draws the future into the present, so that it is no longer simply a 'not yet.' The fact that this future exists changes the present; the present is touched by the future reality, and thus the things of the future spill over into those of the present and those of the present into those of the future" (*Spe salvi* 7). With our hope needing to be lived in the present reality of our daily lives, our Holy Father points out each person's and every family's choice between two approaches to life: either patience, perseverance, and constancy in awaiting the ultimate fulfillment of God's promise, or cowardliness. "For God did not give us a spirit of timidity but a spirit of power and love and self-control" (2 Tim 1:7). It is not always easy to live an unseen reality, especially among all of the various pressures and opportunities for instant gratification that each person in a family encounters. Parents feel the pressures of a consumeristic society, while children experience pressures toward conforming to the "norm" of their peers. As we battle the alluring pleasures of this world, we are not alone as we await our full encounter with God. The Holy Father describes this time on earth as "a looking-forward in Christ's presence, with Christ who is present, to the perfecting of his Body [the Church], to his definitive coming" (*Spe salvi* 9).

The accompaniment of married couples is of paramount importance. We must:

- Be aware of the fact that the future of the Church also depends on the family.
- Help families to meet Christ. The Church does not avail herself of some magic formula or special programs but of the Person of the Lord and of the Gospel. These are her programs, content, and methods.
- Promote communion and friendships among families. Place the spirit of communion above every practical initiative.
- Give space to movements in new communities whose charism is able to bring families together.
- Exploit given opportunities: baptisms, anniversaries ...
- Take advantage of places such as shrines, which offer the opportunity for pilgrimage, the sacrament of reconciliation, the Eucharist, the Rosary, spiritual direction, meetings ... This living tradition keeps the family alive.
- Give importance to Eucharistic adoration. This bears fruits of conversion, and it is the opportunity to rediscover the central role of Christ.
- Discuss the theme of fatherhood and motherhood.
- Encourage witness in the Catholic partner.
- Encourage visits to families by priests: the blessing of families ...
- Walk alongside couples undergoing a crisis.
- Set up permanent itineraries of catechesis.
- Organize pastoral years devoted to families in bishops' conferences and dioceses.

How can we promote good marriages?

In order to promote good marriages, happy families, and a healthy family life, various institutions like the Church, state, and education can be of help.

The Church is crucial here. She must explain the moral law, which is God's plan for marriage and family. She does this from the pulpit and diocesan newspapers and especially in papal documents. She describes what the responsibilities of parenting are. She explains why the dangers to marriage and family life are to be avoided and provides special helps to support good families. She prepares young couples for marriage. She provides religious education for children grades 1–12. She makes available Catholic schools from kindergarten to the university level, where truths of the faith and moral truths are part of the learning experience. She provides classes in Natural Family Planning, family counseling, and pastoral care, especially in the sacrament of reconciliation and forgiveness. She counteracts such contemporary trends as hedonism, abortion, euthanasia, and value-free sex education. Most importantly, she provides the sacraments, whereby every man, woman, and child can obtain the spiritual help he needs to resist temptation, to pursue virtuous living, and to grow in the worship and praise of God.

The Church has both a duty and a right to insure that all the faithful are adequately educated and formed in the Catholic faith, particularly in the areas of chaste living and the Gospel life (*Veritatis splendor* 27–28, 30).

The pastors of the Church under the direction of and in communion with their bishop have a responsibility to serve as models of chaste living for the community as they work to insure that the education and formation of all the faithful in chaste living is in accord with the Church's teaching. This formation includes catechesis on the nature and vocation of men and women created in the image of God and called to form bonds of loving and chaste communion with one another through friendship, service, single life, marriage, and celibacy for the sake of the kingdom (*Gaudium et spes* 49–52) .

Some of the serious duties of a pastor include: providing catechesis for the Christian faithful; instructing and assisting parents and guardians in their role as primary educators of the children in the ways of the faithful consistent with Church teaching; providing formation of those who catechize others—including parents or guardians involved in the catechesis of their children (cf. cann. 528, §1, 773, 776; FC 14).

Marriage is designed by the Creator to promote the good of the spouses and to provide for the procreation and education of children (cf. CCC 2366–67). The openness of conjugal love to life is an urgent aspect to be discovered. We need to increase pro-family and pro-life presence and action: in culture (thought, literature, media), in society (laws, family policies), and in Christian communities (openness to life).

Parents and guardians are to be the first and foremost educators of their children. This God-given responsibility cannot legitimately be taken away by other powers or institutions (CCC 2221; FC 33–34).

Christian parents and guardians are the primary but not the sole educators of their children. They carry out their role in communion with the Church and her pastors who have a responsibility to ensure that the education offered the young is in accordance with Church teaching (*Familiaris consortio* 36, 40). Parents and guardians are assisted by their pastors and the spiritual riches of the Church to receive ongoing Christian formation and to choose the means and institutes that can best promote the Catholic education of their children (*CCC* 2229; *Familiaris consortio* 37) .

The *state* helps by enacting legislation that is pro-family. It provides the material infrastructure that all civil life requires. It does not discriminate against large families or penalize parents of large families through tax structures. It honors and makes possible the parents' right to choose the kind of school their children will attend. It protects the rights of all its citizens, especially the weakest and the unborn. It does not make it financially advantageous for mothers not to marry or for fathers to abandon their families. It establishes good standards for all levels of public education and for public health care.

Public *education* helps promote good marriages and family life by cooperating with parents and Churches in the moral and value formation of students. They help by discouraging anything that weakens the fabric of family, for example, teenage promiscuity, disrespect for legitimate authority, and a disregard for moral principles. All educators in public and private schools must recognize the primary role of parents in education and cooperate with their wishes and directives.

For this reason, preparation for marriage is held in profound respect within the Church. Families themselves sense the serious obligation to prepare the next generation to enter into marriages that are healthy, joyful, and life-giving. In recent times, the Catholic Church has done much to assist families with their role in preparing the next generation for this sacred vocation. Saint John Paul II recognized nearly thirty-four years ago that more extensive marriage preparation programs were needed. In his apostolic exhortation *Familiaris consortio*, he said:

> The changes that have taken place within almost all modern societies demand that not only the family but also society and the Church should be involved in the effort of properly preparing young people for their future responsibilities.... The Church must therefore promote better and more intensive programs of marriage preparation, in order to eliminate as

far as possible the difficulties that many married couples find themselves in, and even more in order to favor positively the establishing and maturing of successful marriages. (*Familiaris consortio* 66)

It is a good thing to encourage future spouses to discover how rich their love should be so that they may understand the dimensions of totality, fidelity, and conjugal chastity. This, in turn, must lead them to understand the definitive character of their own obligation to each other.

Conclusion

If we want to restore good order in marriage and family life, then it is necessary that everyone recall the divine plan and strive to conform to it. Since the greatest obstacle here is intemperate lust, and since we cannot control our passions unless we first subject ourselves to God, this is the approach we take: We must first subject ourselves to God's will. Then, with the aid of his divine grace, we shall be able to subject our passions and their consequences to our mind's good judgments and to our will. Everything else may follow from this. Our task is to offer the love of God to everyone, in whatever family structure they may be. We need to study different family structures thoroughly. This is not to decide which of them are traditional or non-traditional or right or wrong, religious or unreligious. We need to study how best to reach families with Jesus' Good News. This work is God's work. We are invited to join Christ in his mission, and it is a privilege to do so.

The family is both the subject and object of evangelization. In complete harmony with their pastors, parents can carry out better their own duty to evangelize their children, on whom, to a great extent, the evangelization of the family in third millennium depends. With its roots in baptism, the family is a school of adult Christian life. In the family, Christians apply a baptismal priesthood in a particular way. Through the sacraments of initiation, a person's life is fully inserted into the life of the Church, and the foundations of every Christian life are set. Christ acts through the sacraments and asks us to cooperate by preparing our children for these ecclesial events in life.

The family is the privileged place for the transmission of the faith, and it is also a school of prayer. Children are called to progress in the faith and to grow in grace. Baptism, confirmation, and the Eucharist are very important moments in family life. Children must find their principal aid in their parents so that at the end of their adolescence, they will be capable of making a mature choice of Christian life.

With a united effort, we, the priests, deacons, catechists, and laypeople, can encourage our youth, our engaged couples, and our couples already living the magnificent sacrament of marriage to a higher vision of the married vocation. This work of marriage preparation is not for the lukewarm. It is the work of faith-filled disciples, the work of joyful witnesses of Christ. We need to approach this work with all the zeal it calls for, with confidence in our Lord's provision and in the truth as taught by the Church.

Finally, I call each married person to a renewed commitment to love your spouse. God's word reminds us: "A threefold cord is not easily broken" (Eccles 4:12). Life is designed for companionship, not isolation; for intimacy, not loneliness. Neither is God's plan for marriage broken. Marriage vows need not be broken. Seek to understand and embrace God's plan for your life with gratitude. Prepare yourself for a lifelong, exclusive bond of love. Then trust in the Lord. Be not afraid!

The covenant of love that the sacrament of marriage establishes is designed by God to be enriched as years go by. Dear couples, always participate freely and courageously in the grace of this sacrament, so that in the heart of each spouse this Scripture echoes:

> *Set me as a seal upon your heart,*
> *as a seal upon your arm;*
> *for love is strong as death. . . .*
> *Many waters cannot quench love,*
> *neither can floods drown it.*
> (Song of Solomon 8:6–7)

Part Three

Pastoral Care of Families
That Are Hurting

Marriage in Situations of Dysfunction or Weakness

Separation, Divorce, Remarriage

Christian Cardinal Tumi

Introduction

The Christian look that we would like to take at marriage, and particularly at the problems that are the themes of this article, is inseparable from the African that I am. And so for yesterday's and today's African, the notion of family is at the heart of private life; it is a group of persons united by a biological fact (parenthood) and by a juridical act (marriage or adoption). Understood in this way, the family, the basic cell and vital point of all society, has marriage as its immutable foundation. Indeed, from the stable and therefore indissoluble union between one man and one woman, a union that is open to procreation, every family is born. We said "stable", because in our traditions, as also in revelation, people marry for life and not for a time that may be determined by the will of someone besides the contracting parties or by the latter themselves. Today perhaps more than formerly, marriage appears to be a journey, the destination and stability of which are increasingly called into question because of the obstacles encountered along the way. These obstacles most often bear the names of separation and divorce, which can often lead to remarriage. Moreover, what is perplexing is not only the ease with which people decide to separate, to divorce, or even to remarry, but also the ease with which some Africans deny themselves by following the changing winds of fashion.

Christian Cardinal Tumi is archbishop emeritus of Douala, Cameroon.

The project of a book on marriage therefore seems to us salutary more than ever as a way of clarifying again our African concept of marriage and reiterating forcefully and courageously the teaching of the Catholic Church on marriage in general and on Christian marriage in particular. Our article will thus follow the outline of the topic that was proposed to us, addressing one by one the constitutive elements of marriage, then the problems of separation, divorce, and remarriage. These obstacles are numerous, and it will be worthwhile for us to pay very particular attention to them.

I. MARRIAGE: DEFINITION AND ESSENTIAL ELEMENTS

A. Consent

For most of our African traditions and cultures, the conjugal bond is the stable relation by which a man and a woman are united, which results from the fact that they freely committed themselves to one another in order to start a household. This commitment is born of the giving and receiving of what we call consent. Whether it is a question of civil or canon law, the essential element of marriage is consent freely given in full knowledge of the facts. In Africa, too, consent is what makes a marriage, and it consists of two important stages. The first stage in which consent is expressed is the engagement or betrothal. This is of capital importance in traditional marriage. It precedes every marriage and is celebrated after inquiries. It is an institution intended by society to serve as a preparatory school for marriage. The engagement is therefore not the business of the engaged couple alone but also that of the parents. We often hear some say that "African marriage is only a union of bodies", the sole purpose of which is to procreate. But everyone knows that the purpose of the engagement is to teach young people psychological support, mutual affection, and the benefits of service to one another. It seems to us that it is important today to foster this institution and to restore it to its former highly respected status.

The second and final phase of consent is at the time of the wedding itself. The agreement of wills in its initial phase was celebrated at the beginning of the engagement; now it finds its definitive expression.

Consent appears to be necessary for the validity of the conjugal bond, and a more in-depth examination of its nature shows us that marriage takes on an institutional character. In other words, the young people are not going to invent the marriage; there are laws that must be known and obeyed.

From the social perspective, what happens is not that two persons marry, but rather that two families seal their friendship, their union, by this marriage between two of their members. Since it is a question of stability, the various relatives have inquired objectively into the economic, religious, and moral situation of the families of the two future spouses so as to have serious guarantees of the success of the enterprise. There is a real concern for the well-being, the happiness of the girl and the boy. The contract made in this way becomes a legal, social, and political event. In fact, it assures the interests of the clans and of the spouses in different areas; hence its priority and its importance, since the validity of the marriage is at stake. It is true that one might find it ambiguous that there should be a twofold consent, that of the clans and that of the spouses; but the reality is that the consent that makes marriage is the consent between the spouses. Nevertheless, the role of the clans is indispensable in helping the individual understand that he belongs to a group and that he does not live in an airtight container and that the marriage he celebrates is not an individual affair for him to decide arbitrarily.

B. Unity, Indissolubility, and Openness to New Life

Repeating the constant teaching of the Church, the Code of Canon Law states that "the essential properties of marriage are unity and indissolubility, which in Christian marriage obtain a special firmness in virtue of the sacrament" (can. 1056). In other words, once consummated, a valid marriage is indissoluble. But in the case of non-consummation, the law provides that the pope can dispense from a valid marriage.

Marriage, in the context we are examining, is the union between a man and a woman in the sight of God and in the sight of men. It is not about a union between a man and a man or between a woman and another woman. Among the Banso people in Northwestern Cameroon, the Bamileke of the West, or again among the Bakweri of the Southwest and the Bassa people of the Central Region, for example, marriage is a contract, not between two persons, but between two families, two societies, two peoples. Therefore, a woman marries a family and not a man, but she will live her married life with one member of that family. A man marries the family that gave him the woman, but he will live his married life only with his wife. Here marriage is governed by three fundamental laws: indissolubility, openness to fertility, and the unity of marriage.

In Matthew 19, at verse 4, Jesus himself says: "Have you not read that he who made them from the beginning made them male and female, and said, 'For this reason a man shall leave his father and mother and be joined to his wife, and the two shall become one'? So they are no longer two but one. What therefore God has joined together, let no man put asunder." This passage lays bare the law of the unity of marriage, which states that a man may take only one wife; at the same time, it emphasizes the indissoluble character of marriage. Moreover, in the Book of Genesis we read the following: "God created man in his own image, in the image of God he created him; male and female he created them. And God blessed them, and God said to them, 'Be fruitful and multiply, and fill the earth and subdue it'" (1:27). This passage shows that the spouses must be open to fertility.

We find these values of marriage in all matrimonial cultures.

Among Christians, they take on an exceptional value. A ratified and consummated marriage cannot be dissolved by any power or for any reason except death. A ratified but unconsummated marriage can be dissolved by a dispensation granted by the Supreme Pontiff. Since it is a question of the unity of marriage, the conjugal bond is exclusive, so that simultaneous polygamy is, among Christians, by positive divine law, not only illicit but invalid. This thesis affirms three things:

- As long as it lasts, the conjugal bond between two spouses does not allow a new matrimonial contract with a third person;
- Marital union with another wife—if the conjugal bond with the first wife has not been broken—is not only illicit but invalid, in other words, null, nonexistent; the illicitness and invalidity obtain not only by virtue of natural law but also by positive divine law, that is, a law established by Christ himself, the Word of God. Contrary to Martin Luther, the Council of Trent defined as a truth of faith the fact that simultaneous polygamy is illicit by positive divine law.

But we are more interested in the stability of the bond. And so we ask ourselves: Is the indissoluble character of marriage reserved solely for religious marriage? Or else can we say that in God's sight only religious marriage is valid? Our answer is of course negative, inasmuch as every marriage comes from him. Indeed, when a man and a woman decide to join and become husband and wife, they do so in the presence of God, even if they are not Christians and even if they do not know it. The Letter of Saint Paul to the Romans gives us an explanation of this:

> Do you not know, brethren—for I am speaking to those who know the law—that the law is binding on a person only during his life? Thus a married woman is bound by law to her husband as long as he lives; but if her husband dies she is discharged from the law concerning the husband. Accordingly, she will be called an adulteress if she lives with another man while her husband is alive. But if her husband dies she is free from that law, and if she marries another man she is not an adulteress. (Rom 7:1–4)

In this passage, the apostle Paul does not specify that the married woman in question is Christian or a believer. In reality, it is not uncommon to witness in our society the relativization of the notion of marriage. The ease with which one gets rid of the wife or husband whom one has validly married is truly unsettling. This makes us think that even the custom of fear of the Lord has disappeared. Yet he is the author of every marriage, and every valid marriage is sacred.

Thus in the case of Christians, this indissoluble union of marriage is even stronger, because it is a direct representation of the union of Christ and his Church. Christ's union with his Church is indissoluble. The Church is joined to her Lord, to her Husband, her divine Spouse, by a spiritual union and by a physical union. This is the reason why Saint Paul says: "This is a great mystery." In every place where the union is broken, in a couple and in a family, what is broken is the image of the union of Christ and the Church. This is why God attaches such great importance to the couple and to the couple's union. The marital union between a husband and a wife is indissoluble; only death can break it. But this tremendous plan that God prepared for man and woman was disrupted by sin. It often happens that adultery, infidelity ... results in the separation and sometimes the divorce of the spouses.

II. WHY SEPARATION AND DIVORCE?

The *separation* of a married couple is a state resulting from a misunder-standing between the spouses, who, while being married and subject to the obligations of marriage, live separately. It can be temporary, and in this case one may hope for a reconciliation of the spouses.

Divorce is the legal dissolution of a civil marriage, declared by a civil tribunal during the lifetime of the spouses, at the request of one or both spouses according to formalities determined by law. It is also the official break-up of a civil marriage that previously joined two persons, or more in the case of polygamy. In law, a distinction is made between a *de facto* separation without legal consequences and separation from bed and board, which is recognized legally but allows the marriage to remain. This is not to be confused with a declaration of nullity of marriage, which declares that the marriage never took place. If a marriage contracted in Church is not declared null, the Catholic Church does not recognize civil divorce, nor does she foresee any procedure for divorce. Nevertheless, the Church recognizes the possibility, for a serious reason, of a simple separation without remarriage. Divorced persons are there-fore still considered to be married, and a new union of one of them, even if formalized by a new civil marriage, is regarded as adultery.

In order to address the question of separation and divorce, it would be necessary to answer the following questions: What are the true causes within couples of separations and divorces? What is the position of the Catholic Church? In light of the Word of God, what can we do to avoid them, or else how can this kind of situation be managed so that all parties concerned emerge from it satisfied?

Along with the times that we see changing more and more, there are people who wonder whether the Church has changed. In view of the trivialization of marriage, they ask where the Church is headed. Many people who had always heard that a marriage is indissoluble, are led to believe that the Church has changed a lot when they observe the number of cases presented to the ecclesiastical tribunals and the number of declarations of nullity of marriage. Then they hope that they, too, might be able to "get their annulment". And there is no lack of reasons: the spouse was unfaithful and left with the children; the spouse started to drink excessively, to abuse the children, and so on, so that common life became a hell on earth; the spouses discovered, after a few years, that sexual attraction was the only thing that had united them and that actually their personalities were too incompatible for their marriage to succeed and last, and so on.

There are a multitude of reasons for separation and divorce, of which the most common are: adultery, spousal abuse, poverty, the rejection of fertility, the influence of the media on behavior, sterility, the interference of the in-laws in the couple's affairs, and ethnic, religious, and cultural differences.

Adultery is having sexual relations with a person other than one's spouse. This is a serious breach of conjugal duty and of God's law, particularly the Sixth Commandment. In the Book of Malachi, God says that no one should be unfaithful to the wife of his youth, because he hates divorce and anyone who covers his garment with violence. Hence the exhortation to beware and not to be unfaithful (cf. 2:14–17). Adultery is one of the most frequent causes of separation and divorce. In some cultures, particularly that of the Bamilékés, adultery, especially of the wife, is considered a scandal and is fraught with consequences for the wife who has committed adultery. It must be noted, however, that among the Bamilékés, as everywhere else in African societies, the husband's infidelity is tolerated because a Bamiléké man is by nature polygamous. It is not a question here of legitimizing polygamy, because that is a practice contrary to the law of marriage that advocates monogamy. The Book of Genesis says: "Therefore a man leaves his father and his mother and clings to his wife, and they become one flesh" (Gen 2:24). This passage does not suggest that only wives are subject to the law of fidelity but, on the contrary, that spouses are bound to be faithful to each other.

Sterility and the rejection of fertility. These two factors are likewise causes of divorce. Indeed, in African culture, the primary purpose of marriage remains procreation. In couples where the process of procreation is hampered voluntarily or involuntarily, the chances of their marriages lasting until death are greatly reduced. For the Catholic Church, the birth of a child to a couple is not what makes a marriage valid, because the child is a gift from God and not a right of the couple. Besides, it must be noted that the rejection of fertility through the use of contraceptives is still a serious violation of the law of marriage, which wishes the spouses to be ready to accept all the children they can raise decently.

The influence of the media on the behavior of the spouses. In the sphere of globalization, Africans want to live in the Western style, forgetting that we have our own cultural identity and that Western realities are not the same as those of Africa. For example, the images that the media relay to us are generally ones in which marriage is reduced to a trivial contract that can be broken whenever it suits us, in which the notion of head of the family no longer exists because there is equality of the sexes. Nevertheless, in our cultures in Africa, there is a hierarchical arrangement within the couple. The husband is the head of the family, and the wife is mistress of the house. Saint Paul gives directions about the behavior of the husband and wife in marriage:

> Be subject to one another out of reverence for Christ. Wives, be subject to your husbands, as to the Lord. For the husband is the head of the wife as Christ is the head of the Church, his body, and is himself its Savior. As the Church is subject to Christ, so let wives also be subject in everything to their husbands. Husbands, love your wives, as Christ loved the Church and gave himself up for her, that he might sanctify her, having cleansed her by the washing of water with the word, that he might present the Church to himself in splendor, without spot or wrinkle or any such thing, that she might be holy and without blemish. (Eph 5:21–27)

This is not about any "negative" submission, but about the sort that should bring harmony and peace to the couple.

Marital violence. This, too, is at the root of many divorces. At first the violent spouse does not show this side of his personality. Only after the wedding does the mask fall off. In many cases the husband is the one who uses physical violence against his wife. Then, so as not to lose her life, she prefers separation, which most often leads to divorce.

Lack of communication. Communication by a couple is very important, inasmuch as it allows them to dispel misunderstandings and doubts. It helps the spouses to feel that they are not being ignored or neglected but, on the contrary, that there is an attentive ear that listens to them, and most importantly that they are loved.

Interference by in-laws in the couple's affairs and ethnic, religious, and cultural differences. These are recurring situations in Africa. When the mother-in-law lives with the married couple, there is a significant chance that the marriage will end in failure. How many useless quarrels end up killing love! The in-laws, very often, are the ones who show the difference of social class or ethnic group, to the point of creating frustrations for the couple that lead to separation only a few years after the wedding.

Poverty. Although not often mentioned, this is a factor in a not inconsiderable percentage of cases of marital separation. As they say, "When hard times knock at the door, love flees through the window." Nowadays, it is a rare daughter who, after living in luxury and abundance, agrees several years later to live with a poor husband who has been laid off from his job and is going through a difficult time financially.

Besides these well-known causes, we must add sexual dissatisfaction (a source of disagreements and quarrels in bed), sexual impotence, the need for independence, and finally polygamy.

Separation as remedy? The separation of a couple causes many sufferings and even sometimes a feeling of rejection by the people around them, even in a Christian setting. In the Bible, the covenant formed by the husband and wife is considered a gift from God. Each one is therefore urged to do all that he can to live accordingly. However, life together is not always possible, and separation can prove to be a lesser evil in comparison to the excessive sufferings of the couple if they were to continue their common life at all costs. It is a good idea, then, to seek counsel and, in the absence of another viable solution, to consider the decision to separate. Furthermore, separation ought to be the last resort when a couple is having difficulties, as Saint John Paul II told us: "Various reasons can unfortunately lead to the often irreparable breakdown of valid marriages. These include mutual lack of understanding and the inability to enter into interpersonal relationships. Obviously, separation must be considered as a last resort, after all other reasonable attempts at reconciliation have proved vain" (Apostolic Exhortation on the Role of the Christian Family *Familiaris consortio* 83).

Not the separation, but civil remarriage is the thing that the Catholic Church does not accept. Indeed, the commitment that each one made in the presence of God concerning the other in his sacramental marriage continues even in the situation of separation.

III. REMARRIAGE

The expression "divorced and remarried" applies to someone who was married (civilly and possibly religiously) and then divorced and subsequently remarried. Since sacramental marriage is indissoluble, the divorced and remarried are considered in doctrine and in Catholic pastoral practice as living in an irregular situation:

> Reconciliation in the sacrament of Penance, which would open the way to the Eucharist, can only be granted to those who, repenting of having broken the sign of the Covenant and of fidelity to Christ, are sincerely ready to undertake a way of life that is no longer in contradiction to the indissolubility of marriage. (*Familiaris consortio* 84)

Of course the Church must continue to treat divorced persons with care and respect and to offer them real support. But she does not forget that the sacramental bond created by the sacrament of matrimony is not broken by a divorce. Divorce is the dissolution of the civil marriage only. Consequently, a religious remarriage is impossible. It would be contrary to divine law.

Furthermore, the Church encourages separated spouses and divorced persons who have not remarried to stay strong and faithful in prayer, even though that remains very difficult, but not impossible with God's grace: "In such cases their example of fidelity and Christian consistency takes on particular value as a witness before the world and the Church. Here it is even more necessary for the Church to offer continual love and assistance, without there being any obstacle to admission to the sacraments" (*Familiaris consortio* 83).

Conclusion: A pastoral exhortation

For the Church, love must be above all else. Saint Paul says, "Love bears all things" (1 Cor 13:7). Adultery, abandonment of the home, in short, all the reasons that in civil court have legal value and sometimes lead to separation or divorce are in fact accidents that may arrive in the couple's development. Since love is at the basis of everything, when the spouses love one another, they are led to forgive each other and to walk together. Moreover, everything has to be founded on God. Couples who found their love on God and not on self-interest also go through difficult moments. However, these are the couples who hold out. This is an example that all spouses should give: an example of going beyond selfishness and personal interest.

Furthermore, given the ignorance that seems common among some future spouses, marriage preparation ought to be also at the center of pastoral care to the family. It should remind the engaged couple that, in order to be valid, marriage must fulfill three requirements:

- The absence of impediments, for example, consanguinity. . . .
- The completion of the formalities required by canon law, for example, the presence of a priest at the ceremony, or of another legitimately delegated person, who asks for and receives, in the name of the Church, the expression of consent of the two spouses, and also the presence of two witnesses who can vouch for and testify to the manifestation of consent.
- The consent given and received in the presence of the Church is not a waste of time.

Certainly, the usual reason for getting married is love for one another. How could two persons give themselves and accept one another for life, commit themselves to long and difficult plans together, create a community of life that they will want to continue with a family, if they are motivated solely by passion, pleasure-seeking, or a search for novelty? What is necessary in order to enter into a marriage of the sort desired by the Church is a time of reflection, a critical mind that weighs the pros and cons of the engagement, and an autonomous, personal, and entirely free decision.

As the Church sees it, the value of this initial decision is what will determine the legitimacy and validity of the marriage, and only on the basis of this will it be possible to judge later on, in retrospect, whether the marriage entered into was in fact null and invalid, and not on the basis of the disappointments, failures, and even the collapse of some marriages.

In a word, marriage is made for life, for better and for worse. Very often some spouses let themselves be won over by ease, by fear of difficulty, and by a lack of trust in God. One small obstacle is enough for them to change course, whereas the Lord is asking them to persevere, not to flee from the cross. It is true, the lack of a child can be a trial, a cross. But when we look at the story of Abraham and his wife, Sarah, we realize that anyone who places his faith and trust in the Lord always ends up winning his cause; for what is impossible humanly speaking is possible for God.

Monogamy and Polygamy

Challenge and Concern for the Truth of Love in African Cultures

Archbishop Antoine Ganye

Introduction

In discussions about marriage in Africa, world opinion reduces it to structural polygamy. Perhaps it is not mistaken. The practice does exist and is motivated by several reasons. Among others, we might mention the biological infertility of the marriage with the first wife, the desire for numerous offspring,[1] a proof of affluence on the man's part, pride in his virility, the need for plenty of manual labor to work the fields, incompatibility with the first wife, and, finally, the challenge of coping with the inevitability of a high infant mortality rate due to an underdeveloped medical system. Yet in considering these reasons, we can arrive only at the conclusion that polygamy is circumstantial and, therefore, not structural. Rather, monogamy constitutes the first anthropological benchmark at the heart of the marital experience in Africa. It is the foundation of the family, whose mission is to serve love, life, and intergenerational relationships. It is ontologically stable and permanent. Monogamy has good news to proclaim to the world. When the Universal Church

---

Archbishop Antoine Ganye is archbishop of Cotonou.

[1] In Africa it is believed that a child is the greatest treasure. In the culture of Adja-Fon of South Benin, this belief is expressed by the following sentence: "O vi Wɛ nyi le." "Vi dekɔn lɔ zo na ci a." Which can be translated as: The child is the benefit, the most valuable asset, or the best part of a couple. When the child is near the fire, it will not go out.

reflects on family issues, through a synodal process, and seeks to develop new guidelines for the marital stability and spiritual vitality of Christian families, this good news should contribute to the discussion as a set of values. It shows that Africa can be counted on in the common defense of the ideals of marriage and family.

This essay will highlight the foundational cultural elements of monogamy and will mention ad hoc strategies for wider implantation. It will also look at the difficult issue of the baptism of converted polygamists.

1. Foundational Cultural Elements of Monogamy

The very first conviction that emerges from African cultures in relation to the institution of married life is its foundation on the difference between the sexes. In the collective consciousness, marriage, which is the alliance of two families, occurs specifically between a man and a woman. This is what is meant by *alɔ wli wli*, that is, the joining of hands and the sharing of destinies of two persons for love and for life. According to the myths about origins in the culture of Adja-Fon in South Benin, the mystery of the Creator God, called *Mawu Gbɛɖotɔ* or *Sɛgbo Lisa*, was explained as a demiurge couple, which itself manifested the sexual difference (*Mawu*-feminine and *Lisa*-masculine) and created man and woman in its image and gave them to one another. The young married woman is called *Sɛ si*,[2] while her husband is called *Sɛ su*.[3] In both cases, there is the idea that marriage is the result of the woman's gift of herself to the man and the man's gift of himself to the woman. It is the original monogamy. There is one specific man whom God envisions for the woman. There is one specific woman whom God envisions for the man. And he creates the circumstances so that the two can meet, choose each other, and accept each other so as to look in the same direction, live in interpersonal communion, and prepare to welcome and educate children. It sometimes happens that, beyond this first monogamy, polygamy asserts itself.[4] Yet the other wives are still aware that they are not the equals of the first wife. She has her own particular characteristics. This is seen in the manner of referring to her and in her relationship with the other

---

[2] Wife, gift of the Creator.

[3] Husband, gift of the Creator.

[4] Polygamy came about over time due to the manipulation of the semantic field following the disappearance of the foundational text of monogamy.

wives. The first wife is called *Yalé*[5] while the other wives are called *Ha*,[6] *Yao*, or *Yao pɛvi*.[7]

In a lively roundtable discussion of this question, Archbishop Isidore de Souza confirms this institution by citing the research of Sillon Noir, or "Mèwuihouendo", in Benin.[8] He says that, contrary to what is commonly thought, monogamy is the normal way of marriage in black Africa. The proof is that the first wife is considered the legitimate wife because of the name given to her. She is called *Sɛ si*, while the other wives are called *Ha* or *Yao*, that is, concubines, female friends, or co-spouses. She is also considered the only wife destined by the Creator for the man.[9] The other wives themselves are convinced of this. They acknowledge her higher rank and are subject to her. The first wife is the legitimate wife. This legal status is also demonstrated by the "bride price", one of the rites of black African marriage. While the first marriage is accompanied by great solemnity and much involvement of the parents, the marriage of a second or third wife is rather discreet and unobtrusive. The economic burden of these marriages is left up to the man, while for the first marriage, everyone contributes, both financially and in their devotion to the success of the celebration. The same legitimacy is noted in the ritual ceremonies in which she takes her place next to her husband as *Tanyino*, that is, the mistress of ceremonies in worship. It is always up to her to dress her deceased husband. Even if she is separated or divorced, she has the duty to return to the home of her husband to perform the funeral rite, without which the burial cannot take place. She does this because she is the one whom the Creator knows and recognizes as the man's wife. The other co-spouses are only his companions.

All these elements just mentioned demonstrate that in the collective consciousness, marriage is monogamous by nature and only gives way to polygamy contingently. And even though polygamy seems pervasive,

[5] The first true and legitimate spouse.

[6] Female friend or concubine.

[7] The little wife who does not have the same dignity as the first. The first wife's dignity comes from the fact that she is the predestined and truly God-given one. The others are personal conquests of the man for one reason or another.

[8] "Mèwuihouendo" (in French, Sillon Noir) is a movement for inculturation founded by Bishop Barthélemy Adoukonou.

[9] See Archbishop Isidore de Souza, "Table ronde sur le Mariage et la famille", in *Revue de l'Institut Catholique de l'Afrique de L'Ouest* 5–6 (1993): 164.

monogamy does not cease to be the social priority. In a carefully written, well-documented book, the Togolese priest Pidalani Pignan reports on a sociological study done by the physician Jean-Claude Froelich on the question of marriage statistics among the populations of North Togo. This study shows that Africans in general, and the Togolese in particular, have, by nature, a monogamous mentality. Marriage becomes polygamous only because of circumstances, especially due to the desire for children, who are considered a blessing and a guarantee of posterity. When the first, predestined wife proves to be infertile, the husband calls on other women or concubines to ensure fertility. In this regard, the study shows that on average 70 percent of marriages are monogamous, 24.7 percent bigamous, 5.3 percent polygamous, and that there are 7.18 children per family.[10] That says it all. African countries, with the exception of Muslims, like monogamy and want to preserve it. Today, this desire for monogamy is observed increasingly in young people living in urban areas. While it is true that monogamy becomes imperative due to economic necessity and the requirements of responsible fatherhood, it does not fail to agree with a basic belief that the woman wants to have one husband, and the husband, one wife. God grant that this desire for monogamy may remain in the hearts of young people and will have a greater sphere of influence. In order to do this, the pastoral work of the Church is expected to awaken and solidify in people's consciences what nature has already sown and what the culture has confirmed and sometimes questioned. This awakening cannot take place without the implementation of ad hoc strategies.

2. Strategies for Spreading Monogamy in Africa

The very first strategy is formation by means of information about the advantages and consistency of monogamy.

a. The advantages of monogamy

The adoption of monogamy has spiritual, psychological, familial, and economic advantages.

---

[10] See J.-C. Froelich, *Les populations du Nord-Togo* (Paris: PUF, 1963), 66. Cited by P. Pignan, *Le mariage chrétien et le mariage traditionnel Kabiyè à la lumière de l'enseignement du concile Vatican II* (Paris: Éd. Sogico, 1987), 81.

At the spiritual level, it is important to explain to young people that choosing monogamy is consistent with the Creator's design for marriage and is proof of their love for God. When we love God, we do his will.

At the psychological level, they will know that fulfillment in life comes from oneness in being and in the state of being. This is so true that a philosopher once said, "If man was one, he would never be ill." Unity is one of the transcendentals of the human being. To seek unity in all life's choices is the true path to well-being. Scattering has never fulfilled the human being. Instead, it tears him apart and eventually dismantles him. With regard specifically to married life, it is truly fulfilling only in the context of monogamy and in the commitment that each spouse makes to meet the other's expectations. It can happen that, due to selfishness and the failure to perceive each other's expectations, monogamy does not provide the expected happiness. Even if that were the case, it would be better to maintain monogamy. Therein is found the truth of conjugal love. Furthermore, a man becomes unified and completely fulfilled with one wife rather than by being scattered among several. With one wife, the duties and worries are one. With several, a man multiplies his worries as well as his problems. The young man must pay attention to this if he really wants to set out in a beneficial direction. Being monogamous has its advantages.

At the family level, we can see another advantage, that of stability and harmony. Children who have had the unfortunate experience of living in the heart of a polygamous family are not ready to replicate this model. Besides the fact that polygamy creates rivalry between the wives, it leads to conflicts among the children. They do not have the same chances of success. And if ever the additional problems of inheritance and obscurantism crop up, it is a complete catastrophe. It may happen that the polygamist himself puts on airs and seems to be a happy and influential man. It is only a façade. No! Polygamy is not a model of conjugal life to be replicated. It is more a brood of problems than a path to happiness. A flourishing family is one in which a community of children is not only gathered around one father and one mother but is also introduced to intergenerational communion. The biblical writer proclaims the beauty of this when he tells the husband: Your wife will be like a fruitful vine within your house; your children will be like olive shoots around your table.[11] It is both vitally important and vitalizing to be exposed to such

---

[11] See Ps 128:3.

a family model. It is advantageous not only for the couple but also for the children.

Economically, there are many advantages to monogamy as well. Besides being the setting in which to experience the truth of love, the family is also the place of economic support. In the African tradition, it is primarily the husband who takes care of his wife and children. The responsibility for the food, the health care, the education and all sorts of training for each one is no less his. He must have the means to deal with it. This, incidentally, is why some young people delay marriage. With a wife and children, it is not easy. And when there are several wives, it is even more complicated. The happy family is the one that finds its stability in spiritual, emotional, psychological, and economic balance. Polygamy does not usually embrace this model. Nor does it correspond to the consistency of marriage.

b. The consistency of monogamy with conjugal love

The consistency of marriage is found in monogamy. There are anthropological and theological arguments to support such an assertion.

By its nature and in principle, marriage is defined as a covenant of stable love between a man and a woman. These are the ones whom we named earlier Sε su and Sε si. Each one is convinced of it. That is why, when one feels the desire for marriage awakening in one's heart, one turns to the beloved to form a partnership of life with her or him. From then on, each one exists for the other. One is so fond of the beloved as to be ready to show jealousy when he becomes the object of attention of other persons who wish to snatch him away. Anthropologically, this jealousy shows that in conjugal love, one does not share a spouse but rather keeps that person for oneself. One supports a spouse and cares for him and makes him happy. The truth of conjugal love is found in monogamy.

Monogamy like this also has an ontological-legal consistency that reveals both the equal dignity of the husband and the wife and their obligation to ensure the rights and duties that result from their marriage. Just as the wife is entitled to one husband, the husband should be entitled to a single wife. To take several is to ignore the wife's equal dignity and disperse the rights that belong exclusively to her. Polygamy is a lack of consideration for women. It is the negation of their dignity. It is essentially an attack on the wife as a human being and on her rights.

It is not consistent with the natural idea of marriage and contradicts what is taught by the Bible and theology.

"Male and female he created them", the sacred author declares. In this statement, there are two truths that appear as the essential characteristics of conjugal love: sexual difference and monogamy. Conjugal love cannot be adapted to a couple of the same sex; it is coherent only in the unity of sexual difference. This is no accident. In the arrangements of Divine Providence, each sex, with its own particular characteristics, has gifts to give the other. It is at the same time a gift and a source of fulfillment for the other. The account of the divine institution testifies to this when it says that at the sight of the created woman, the man cried: "This at last is bone of my bones and flesh of my flesh."[12]

Pope John Paul II, commenting on this passage, sees in it the beginning of human happiness on earth.[13] It flourishes in the *communio personarum*. But beyond this communion, there is also another purpose for which God gives a woman to a man and a man to a woman. Primitive Adam prophetically expressed this when he called the woman "Eve", that is to say, the mother of the living. The woman is given to the man as a source of happiness and fertility. God himself confirmed this when he said "Be fruitful multiply, and fill the earth and subdue it."

Within the scope of marriage, there was originally the mission of joyful communion, open to the culture of life. This is what the Bible teaches. It is true that the rest of the story about marriage showed that events took a different turn. The advent of sin has indeed changed the relationship of communion into a relationship of domination and possession. This desire to dominate has been and remains the source of all the tragedies that have occurred in the experience of married love: infidelity, divorce, polygamy, and murder. It took the arrival of the true Bridegroom, Christ, to reestablish the truth about conjugal love.

As part of accomplishing the mission of salvation entrusted to him by his Father, Christ assumed all of humanity and gave himself to her as a bridegroom should normally give himself to his bride, in keeping with the original concept. The apostle Paul championed this reality in these words: "Christ loved the church and gave himself up for her."[14]

---

[12] See Gen 2:18–24.

[13] John Paul II, *Man and Woman He Created Them: A Theology of the Body*, trans. Michael Waldstein (Boston: Pauline Books and Media, 2006), 158–60.

[14] See Eph 5:25.

He loved the one Bride that his Father gave him. He did not balk at the sacrifices and sufferings that often destroy homes. He remained faithful despite the infidelity of his Bride, the Church. Therefore, he was not only the source of her joy but also the means of her fruitfulness. The apostle Paul, contemplating this wonder, recommends it to the Christian couples of his time saying: "Husbands, love your wives, as Christ loved the Church.... This is a great mystery, and I mean in reference to Christ and the Church."[15] The term "mystery" that is used here is rendered in Latin by another word, *sacramentum*, which means sign and symbol. Paul's intention in using this word is to invite the Christians of his communities to live in the type of marital relationship that is a continuation of the model that is visible in Christ. In other words, if a Christian couple has already found in the nature of marriage a direction for life, it is above all in the contemplation of Christ's redeeming love that the couple will find the ultimate model, with the commitment to perpetuate it for life. It is even more imperative that the couple be Christian. In baptism, a man becomes a son in the only Son. But in marriage, he becomes a husband in the manner of Christ the Bridegroom, assuming all the attributes belonging to him. In his encyclical letter *Humanae vitae*, Pope Paul VI strongly emphasizes this. He speaks of the unity, humanity, exclusivity, totality, fertility, and indissolubility of conjugal love.[16] These are the areas on which the Christian couple is called to work so that their marriage is consistent with the fact that they belong to Christ through baptism. The young Christian who wants to marry today must not try to do without this existential consistency.

Actually, young people do believe in it and accept it. However, some of them have not been spared the effects of divorce and polygamy. Ordinarily, divorce comes as a response to marital difficulties, and polygamy, as a remedy for infertility. This is also one of the major problems challenging the African Christian couple, despite their willingness to be faithful to the ideal of Christian marriage. Indeed, in a world where procreation is considered to be the very first purpose of marriage, some spouses without children have the impression that their marriage has no meaning. In this perspective, it becomes difficult to practice marital

---

[15] See Eph 5:25, 32.
[16] See Paul VI, encyclical *Humanae vitae* 9.

fidelity despite the goodwill to maintain it. And yet, one should resolve to do so by remembering that the essential mission of the marriage is the realization of love. The child is a gift from God. And God gives the child in God's own way: whether biologically or by adoption. The future Christian husband must be imbued with this reality so as not to go down paths that are contrary to the Gospel truth.

In other words, even though monogamy may be subject to the challenges of the times, it deserves to be maintained because of its consistency with nature and with faith. This is the message that young Africans must hear, receive, and practice. They will welcome it more readily if they are inspired by the radiant witness of experienced Christian couples. And even if it should happen that this testimony is unconvincing, it can never be used as a pretext to veer off the correct path. The truth of love is found in monogamy.

However, this obvious fact is not welcomed by all. Although a young man who is single and informed can easily reconcile himself with the ideal of monogamy, the question still remains for a pagan who is already polygamous. How can we help introduce him to monogamy and thus give him access to the sacraments of the Church? This a problem that challenges the pastoral ministry of the Church. How can it be resolved without leaving a large number of people outside the Christian faith? This is a major question to which we must find answers.

3. The Challenge of Christian Marriage for Polygamous Pagans

a. The Magisterium's position on this subject

The problem is not new. It is well known that since the sixteenth century it has been an object of concern for the Church, although she has been unable to find a sufficiently decisive response. The most recent response in this regard is the one given by the 1983 Code of Canon Law in canon 1148, which states:

> After he has received baptism in the Catholic Church, a previously non-baptized man who simultaneously has several non-baptized wives can keep one of them as his wife while dismissing the others if it is difficult for him to remain with the first. The same is true for a non-baptized woman who simultaneously has several non-baptized husbands....

After considering the moral, social and economic situation of area and of the persons, the local ordinary is to take care that sufficient provision is made in accord with the norms of justice, Christian charity and natural equity for the needs of the first wife and of the other wives who are dismissed.

Actual practices show that this canon is not easy to apply. One may be startled, first, by the language that puts an end to the ties with the wives not chosen by the converted polygamist. The term used is "dismissed". No doubt it makes sense in terms of the law, but it shows a lack of sensitivity to the person who is being "dismissed". How can a woman who has never thought about separating from the husband she loves be forced to give up everything from one day to the next and to fend for herself in solitude, while the husband continues to live a fulfilling married life with the chosen wife?[17] How is this solution acceptable if the dismissed wife continues to love the husband who has dismissed her? How is this solution acceptable if the dismissed wife no longer has assets to her name with which to enter into a new marriage? What will be her future? What will be the future of her children, since we know that they, too, need the father figure for their upbringing?

We will leave these questions unanswered and simply say that, in practice, the application of this canon results in implicit hatred toward the chosen wife and creates conflicts between the children whose mother is chosen and those whose mothers are dismissed. Repeatedly it has been observed that the children in the second group are opposed to their father's marriage in the Church. These are facts that prompt some theologians and pastors to look at this solution with some perplexity. Can we in fact, in the name of faith, create situations of injustice at the family level? It is true that some dismissed wives have consented to the arrangement and taken advantage of it to regularize their situation so that they, too, could receive the Eucharist. Nevertheless, this does not remove the perplexity connected with the practice. To overcome this, several pastoral proposals have been made. It would be interesting to discuss them here and to interpret them critically, before retaining what might seem to be most feasible in reality.

---

[17] Here it is important to note that, in some situations, this procedure is not a problem, since the wives gather together to choose the one who will participate in the religious ceremony with their converted spouse.

b. Pastoral proposals for the baptism of polygamists

On the basis of the view that polygamy is the paradigm for marriage in Africa, some theologians and pastors think that there is no need to impose monogamy on polygamists. If they wish to receive baptism, they can do so while remaining polygamists. Moreover, accepting them for baptism would increase the number of Christians in the communities. What are we to think of such a proposal?

Before examining it, we should note that consideration of polygamy as the model of marriage in Africa reflects a misunderstanding of African anthropology. In this regard, we have already said that the African is essentially monogamous. He becomes polygamous only for circumstantial reasons, the most significant of which is his first wife's infertility. In Africa, a house without children is like a day without sunshine. The child is the fruit of the marriage. When the legal wife cannot have children, the husband often calls on another wife. This is bigamy. The above-cited sociological surveys of Dr. Froelich have proven it. Talking about "African marriage" in terms of polygamy is to make an unwarranted caricature of Africa.

That being said, it must be noted that baptism is the seal of faith in the God of Jesus Christ. This faith has its ethics. It has its requirements. And one of them is the conversion that leads a person to go from one state to another, especially from profligacy to a more consistent way of life. As for marriage, monogamy is the ideal that corresponds to God's design. To receive baptism while turning aside from this ideal is to act as if baptism had accomplished nothing in our life.

Moreover, it is difficult to understand the reasoning that seeks to legitimize the baptism of polygamous pagans, arguing that this will increase the number of Christians in Africa since there are many polygamists. In this regard, it is important to note one thing. Before gaining large numbers, thanks to the influence of her mission and the witness of Christian lives, the Church's policy is always to start with a small number of credible, qualified, and proper Christians. Thanks to the integrity of this small number, a large number are called and challenged. This is both biblical and historical. In the Bible, this perspective is in keeping with God's teaching method. Indeed, we speak about the small remnant of Joseph from which everything became full of promise for the future. In the history of the Church, there is no lack of illustrations of this perspective.

In trying times, the faithfulness and the martyrdom of the small number always assured the coming of a great number of qualified Christians in the future. Faith requires conversion, transformation, and transfiguration. It is unacceptable to make Africans second-rate Christians. The Christian faith has its own ethics, and African ethics must correspond to it. All the more reason because Africa already has the seeds of the Word in its culture. With regard to everything that has just been said, it should be clear that the proposal that seeks to let the polygamist remain in polygamy and receive baptism objectively contradicts the requirements of the Christian faith.

Another proposal is to ask the polygamists to follow the catechumenate, at the conclusion of which the Church will give them a sacramental instead of the sacrament of baptism. This sacramental, which consists of a special blessing, will enable them to be incorporated into the Christian community while living their lives apart from the sacraments. What are we to think of this proposal? It certainly appeases polygamists who are far from the Church and desire to enter. But the solution is not ideal. It is not a sacramental or a blessing that gives access to the Church but, rather, the sacrament of baptism. Baptism makes us sons and daughters in the "only Son Jesus Christ" and assures our inclusion in the family of God's children. To make a sacramental, a mere blessing, the way of entering the Church is to attribute to it a privilege that it does not have. The worst thing is that this may lead to confusion and even give the polygamist the impression that he no longer has to make any effort to convert. This is very dangerous. Faith must be expressed by going beyond one's former imperfect situation. The polygamist needs to adopt this perspective. If, for now, the polygamist cannot, the Church's pastoral practice will have to become more creative in order to find a *modus vivendi* that is more appropriate for the Church and more suitable for the polygamist's state of life. In this way we can break the impasse.

c. Breaking the impasse

To break the impasse is to make proposals that agree with the ideal of Christian marriage: monogamy. A polygamist who wants to receive baptism must force himself to accept it. In this connection, the requirement stated in canon 1148 of the 1983 Code of Canon Law is universally welcome: the selection of one of the wives and the dismissal of the others. Nevertheless, for the psychological, moral, familial, and economic well-being of the wives who are not chosen, this canon can very well be adapted to a more realistic pastoral practice. By doing what? The polygamist, after choosing one wife for Christian marriage, will indicate the end of his intimate relations with the others by moving them to houses that he has built or rented for them and for their children. However, if he does not have the means with which to do that, he may be permitted to keep living in the same house with the wives not chosen and their children. Only the chosen wife will cohabit with him. The other wives will be considered "free women": free of any marital commitment, free to leave the house if they want, and above all free to rearrange their sacramental situation. Such a proposal is similar to the concession made by John Paul II to the divorced and remarried in relation to their access to the sacraments. While staying in the same house, they can go to Communion under certain conditions. He speaks of this in the Post-Synodal Apostolic Exhortation *Familiaris consortio*:

> When, for serious reasons, such as for example the children's upbringing, a man and a woman cannot satisfy the obligation to separate, they "take on themselves the duty to live in complete continence, that is, by abstinence from the acts proper to married couples".[18]

The solution for the polygamist's situation can follow the same lines as this concession. But precautions must be taken so that this state of life does not lead to scandal within the Christian community. All the Christians of the community must be informed about it so as to have an exact understanding of it. However, if this course of action would be dubious, for one reason or another, it must be avoided. One must take into account the common sense of the faithful and their spiritual and psychological maturity. From this perspective, it will be up to the local Ordinary to gauge whether this solution is opportune. He will see to it that this pastoral approach avoids all confusion that could lead anyone to think that, generally speaking, polygamy is now recognized and legitimate within the Catholic Church. In 1978, the Fifth General Assembly of the Symposium of Episcopal Conferences of Africa and Madagascar

---

[18]John Paul II, apostolic exhortation *Familiaris consortio* 84.

(SECAM) drew attention to this in these terms: "We feel compassion for persons who strongly desire baptism and the sacraments but have contracted polygamous marriages following the local custom and in good faith.... (Nevertheless) the pastoral attitude toward polygamists must avoid anything that could appear to be recognition of polygamy by the Church."

It is important, therefore, to be cautious about proposals and actions that could manipulate the Christian faith by watering it down to suit current tastes or the perversions of the culture. Although the sacrament of baptism is a door of salvation, one must also face the self-evident fact that salvation is not reduced to the sacrament. God has broader views and meets each of his children in a way peculiar to him. From this perspective, the polygamist can indeed attain salvation without, however, receiving baptism and being incorporated into the Christian community. Saint Augustine, one of the glories of African Christianity, expresses this conviction well in these terms: "Many who seem to be on the outside (pagans) are in fact on the inside, and many who seem to be on the inside (of the Church) are nevertheless in fact on the outside." The spiritual difference is that the former have a love that transforms them and causes them to live a good life. Saint John of the Cross teaches us that on the last day we will be judged by that love.

Conclusion

In conclusion, we can say that, in the current state of affairs, the most appropriate solution is for the Church to continue her work of accompanying polygamists, even if they do not receive the sacraments. She will make it her mission to accompany them patiently, compassionately, and perseveringly. She will dedicate to this mission ad hoc structures allowing them to feel sympathetic toward the Church because of the sympathy of her pastors toward them.

But it seems even more urgent to work pro-actively, among African children and young people, to teach them to love marital love in its monogamous form. Here, the pastoral ministry of the Church is called upon to meet them in their houses, in the parishes, in the schools, in the universities, and in all places of formation. It must be possible to organize on their behalf a catechesis of love that will make them abandon emotional illiteracy and lead them to the truth of the matter. By sowing in advance and by organizing a serious pastoral program of marriage and family, we will truly help Africans live according to an ethics of married life that corresponds authentically to nature and to the faith. This is the challenge. It must become a pastoral concern everywhere. There is a vast field of work ahead. We must begin now.

The Challenge of Mixed and Interfaith Marriages

Théodore Adrien Cardinal Sarr

Introduction: Faith in the family, love of the family

We take the challenge posed by mixed and interfaith marriages to be one of the great challenges confronting the Church in Africa, one of the major issues facing Christ's faithful in matters of pastoral care to the family and one we are adding to the dossiers of the synod on the family.

Like life, and together with it, the family is the thing that an African holds most dear, in his specific culture, in the sense of his way of seeing the world and of recognizing himself and developing in it. Outside of his family and his more or less extended social environment, an African generally finds his way with greater difficulty. When he ends up elsewhere, disorientation and anonymity may get the better of his humanity.

Moreover, we have a great reason for joy and for pride in Africa: here the people still unanimously share the sense and the vision of the family as a community of life between a man and a woman (heterosexual human beings), open to children, into which they publicly enter through marriage. This is a large common foundation, on which the spouses can build a family, whatever their ethnic groups, their peoples, their countries and nations, their cultures, their religions may be.

More and more we can observe that the desire to marry, a response to the vocation to marriage, is so strong in some individuals that it tries to break racial, cultural, social, and religious barriers.... We can rejoice in this as a manifestation of love that is stronger than any obstacle.

By *mixed marriage*, we mean, in keeping with canon law, marriage between a Catholic party and a party belonging to a non-Catholic

Théodore Adrien Cardinal Sarr is archbishop emeritus of Dakar.

Christian denomination. By *interfaith marriage*, we mean marriage between a Catholic party and a non-baptized party, a marriage that canon law calls *disparate marriage*.

In the answers to *question 39* of the *Relatio synodi*, the distinction between mixed marriages and interfaith or disparate marriages is made clearly. A group of laymen from the Commission for Priestly and Religious Vocations of the Archdiocese of Dakar clearly recognizes that, in order to contract a mixed or disparate marriage, the Catholic party needs an explicit dispensation by the competent ecclesial authority, whether it is a question of a dispensation for mixed marriage or a dispensation of disparity of cult for a disparate marriage.

The group writes:

> *A mixed marriage* is a marriage between two Christians of different confessions. Here, ecumenism advocates the unity of Christians around Christ (Gal 3:28–29), so that among baptized persons there is a common spiritual legacy. Provided that the faith and dogmas of each party are respected, this type of marriage is more acceptable, despite everything (cf. can. 755, §1–2; cann. 1124–25; *Ut Unum sint*, 97.1).
>
> A *"disparate marriage"* is celebrated thanks to a dispensation for disparity of cult, since this is a marriage between a Catholic party and a non-baptized party. Without this dispensation, such a marriage is invalid. Its acceptance by means of the dispensation for disparity of cult has gradually become easier in the context of dialogue in all its forms (in particular the dialogue of life and of charitable works) between monotheistic believers.

Nevertheless, the dangers of abandoning the Catholic faith and of abdicating one's duty as a believing Catholic to educate and even to baptize one's children in the Catholic faith, on the one hand, and, on the other hand, the fact that the non-baptized party, for cultural or religious reasons, may not know the ends and properties of Catholic marriage oblige the parties to conduct a serious examination before making such a decision.

Indeed, despite declarations of intention and commitments, the record of intra- and extra-marital crises, which often enough end in apostasy, demands that the Catholic Church be very strict about this sort of marriage. Indeed, one fear will always be present: Will the non-baptized party, even though monotheistic in his beliefs, accept for the rest of his life the concept of marriage built on *freedom, fidelity, unity, indissolubility, respect for fertility*, and *openness to new life*?

Not one but several challenges

- The first challenge posed by mixed and interfaith marriages, as well as by marriages between Catholics, is the challenge of *the evangelization of the African family*. It confronts all baptized Africans: how to build families that remain authentically African while becoming authentically Christian families.

- In addition to this first challenge, in mixed marriages and especially in interfaith marriages, there is the challenge of undertaking *a Christian witness and apostolate in marital and familial life*. Ecumenism and interreligious dialogue are not optional for Catholics. They are two specific challenges, and it is necessary to find strategies for a response to the duty of mission.

- Then we have the challenge of the permission that must be requested and obtained for mixed marriage or of the dispensation for disparity of cult that must be requested and obtained for disparate marriages. This is a challenge that confronts the petitioners as well as their pastors.

1. The Challenge of Proclaiming the Gospel of Marriage and the Family in Africa

Only an African family that has been evangelized, in the sense of *Evangelii nuntiandi* (*EN*) 17–24, will be more and more a place for the birth and formation of men and women who have the Christian prudence that is indispensable for commitment in the adventure of a mixed or interfaith marriage. Such families will belong to milieus where not only individual persons are converted to Christ, but the culture, too, is converted.

This work, no doubt, is described well in *EN* 18 and 19, but the task to be carried out is immense. Let us listen to Pope Paul VI:

> For the Church, evangelizing means bringing the Good News into all the strata of humanity, and through its influence transforming humanity from within and making it new: "Now I am making the whole of creation new."[1] (*EN* 18)

> Strata of humanity which are transformed: for the Church it is a question not only of preaching the Gospel in ever wider geographic areas or to

[1] Rev 21:5; cf. 2 Cor 5:17; Gal 6:15.

ever greater numbers of people, but also of affecting and as it were upsetting, through the power of the Gospel, mankind's criteria of judgment, determining values, points of interest, lines of thought, sources of inspiration, and models of life, which are in contrast with the Word of God and the plan of salvation. (*EN* 19)

Of course there are some African family realities to convert, because they are "in contrast with the Word of God and the plan of salvation". But man, under whatever skies he may live, is nothing but a contrast with the Word of God and the plan of salvation. Therefore he is also the bearer of values to be adopted, corrected, and transfigured.

In this regard, Saint Paul can be consulted. Indeed, how many times does he exhort the disciples of Christ to set themselves apart from the prevailing ways in their societies by allowing themselves to be transformed by the renewal of their mind so as to seek God's will and what pleases him (Rom 12:2). At the same time, he recommends to them, through his letter to the Christians in Philippi, to keep and cultivate the values of society: "Finally, brethren, whatever is true, whatever is honorable, whatever is just, whatever is pure, whatever is lovely, whatever is gracious, if there is any excellence, if there is anything worthy of praise, think about these things" (Phil 4:8). He calls for fraternal charity in particular to dwell in the hearts of believers (Heb 13:1), who must hate evil, with sincere charity (Rom 12:9). Therefore it is necessary to fight systematically against divisions (1 Cor 1:11), as well as jealousy and strife (1 Cor 3:3), by helping one another along these lines (Rom 12:10).

What emerges from these biblical references is the possibility of keeping ancestral usages and customs that in no way infringe on the Catholic faith and come under the heading of inculturation. This is in keeping with the mission of Christ, who came to fulfill and not to abolish. As salt of the earth and chosen from the midst of the world (Jn 15:19), Catholics ought to love one another (Jn 13:35), especially their peers.

Saint Peter, for his part, exhorts Christ's faithful to conduct themselves honorably in the world, so as to silence critics and to lead all to praise God (1 Pet 2:11–12).

Although the need to *correct* is urgent, so too is the need to *transfigure the traditional values of the African family*, which the Teams of Our Lady (*Équipes Notre-Dame*) of Senegal point out in a document dealing with "African Values and Christianity" and "Values Adopted by the Senegalese".

They write about these two questions:

The African Christian family, which is capable of making a new world in a new Africa, is the institution capable of integrating the positive values of traditional Africa by rediscovering all the values and strengths of the continent through inculturation. In particular these are:

The covenant by which two individuals, or rather two persons, form a relationship of sharing and kinship and, by that very fact, influence families, groups, communities, cultures, by summoning them to observe Jesus Christ's law of love. This is the reason why the family, unity in plurality, is a beautiful thing! How insipid and somber life would be if there were no covenant, no dialogue, no encounter, no discovery of another, of every human being in the image of God, Father, Love, Savior, and Creator of the whole universe.

Relationship in the family is fraternity offered by the one God, Creator and Savior, through love in Jesus Christ and in the Spirit, love cast like a net throughout the world and its creatures. This prompts Saint Francis of Assisi to say, when he speaks about animals and creatures, "my brothers, my brother the ass, the wolf. . . ."

This is the same idea that also prompts the Sérère wise man to say through this song of the initiates: "The little circumcised boy holds the hand of the *Selbé* (his instructor), who in turn hold the hands of the *Kuma* (his Teacher), who holds the hand of the King, who grasps the hand of God!" What a good and beautiful thing kinship is! "*O fog soom felu*", the Sérère says: "How good and beautiful is kinship!"

Solidarity, this tie, this natural instinct that drives us toward the other, is explained by the fact that we are twofold, or rather threefold, for "there are never two without three." Every human being, every person is another self; my child is the child of my brother or of my sister. Well then, since we experience solidarity in being alive, we must practice solidarity toward others. This is even more true within the same family; now we are all sons or daughters of the one family of God and of his children, all men, of every race, creed, or social condition.

Respect for elders, those who have traced the furrows of the testimony and wisdom of ancestors, the founders of lines and generations: "Honor thy Father and thy Mother."

We live in an age in which the respect due to elders is diminishing and even disappearing. "Democracy obliges", some shortsighted people will say, who think only of efficiency and their selfish interests. This unjust concept must be banished, for an elder is a gift of God to younger persons, and disrespect toward elders is a sin, a lack of solidarity, love, and support for the weakest (for the elder and the aged person who is still alive). God has a promise in store, says the Sérère proverb. This promise may be a great good, a gift for the younger sibling and younger generations.

Veneration of ancestors, without whom we would have no models or heritage, without which we are as light as a tree leaf in the wind.

I exist through my ancestors, because of them!

The veneration of ancestors is a filial duty. The blood that flows in the veins of a son or a daughter, the heart or the mind, the judgment or the intellect, the soul or the spirituality that shape a man or a woman, come also from their ancestors, to whom God entrusted a life and talents so that they might transmit them to their descendants. How then can we not venerate these ancestors who certainly watch over us through love!

The kind of hospitality that welcomes the other, who is another self, who is Christ in need of being housed, fed, clothed, loved, and helped—who is my brother. You know this page from the Gospel. My brother and my sister are blood relatives who are close to me, but also those who are close in heart and mind in the family, the neighborhood, the community, the county, the state or region, the nation, the continent, the world, close because of culture, creed, or spirituality. It is "a man" (who once was going down from Jerusalem to Jericho) about whom the Gospel speaks. For me, too, that man can be a Wolof, Peul, Susu, Diola, Sérère, Tukulor [ethnic groups in Senegal], Christian, Muslim, any other believer, any other man or woman of good will! He can even be my enemy, my adversary! Who is my brother? Who is my mother? Who is my father?

Dialogue and speech enable us to be open to the other and make possible encounter, the exchange of fraternity among persons, families, groups, and structures, inside and outside. Speech or dialogue is sometimes decried, and yet for what purpose did God give us a mouth, a tongue, roads and paths to meeting places? To dialogue, to speak, to converse, to make a lot of noise! These are moments and encounters of peace and fraternity. Senghor [a Senegalese scholar and politician] was right to theorize and to write poetry about the Dialogue-Word!

Time, which is a gift from God and enables us to be born, to grow, "to learn how to be acquainted, to do, to be, to communicate and to live together!" It is precious; time is money, they say. No doubt it can be; but money slips away and is lost. Time is there, it comes and goes and remembers. It is eternal. "The dead are not dead" (Birago Dio, Senegalese poet).

Man the person, created in the image of God, "man's remedy" (a Senegalese expression), guardian of his brother, father or mother of man, son of God, finite but tending toward the infinite, toward eternity!

Truly, armed with all these ancestral values, once they have been freed from the dregs, the parasites, and the burdens that are paralyzing antivalues and washed by the purifying waters of Christ in the Jordan, Christians are saved; but they are often afraid, intimidated! With more faith and courage, they can save the world. There were twelve who followed Christ. And how many are there today?

The great challenge is to become truly Christian! To become and to form authentically Christian families! "If we had faith the size of a mustard seed, we could move mountains!" Yes! The great challenge is to become authentically African and Senegalese Christian families. What great, beautiful challenges to meet! Yes! To become authentically African and Senegalese, while integrating the positive and humanistic values of our civilizations.

By the Teaching Teams of Senegal

This challenge confronts all baptized persons, particularly all those who respond to the vocation to marriage and take up the mission of marriage.

2. The Challenge of Mixed and Interfaith Marriages

The challenge posed by mixed marriages and interfaith marriages can therefore be transformed into a challenge to evangelize by Catholic lay faithful who have come from "authentically Christian African families", yet must live out the Gospel in close proximity to non-Catholics. Such members of Christ's lay faithful will be increasingly capable of devising the *strategies for mission* that we call *ecumenism* and *interreligious dialogue*.

We should explain that when we say "strategy", we are not talking about "proselytism", but rather the ability and strength to share one's conviction about the Catholic belief in Jesus Christ, in whom God became one of us so that we might become divinized (see Saint Leo the Great).

Given the difficulties of the present-day human condition, and given the doubt about a happy outcome of this condition, it is a matter of knowing how to share one's faith-conviction that in the Risen Jesus Christ another form of human life is given to every human being and that we all attain it, beyond our differences, even religious ones, if we love as God loves us, placing ourselves at the service of our brethren by our efforts to be kind and charitable.

Beyond our differences, even religious ones: we must listen to Saint John Paul II on this subject:

> In the light of this mystery (this radiant mystery of the unity of the human race in its creation and of the unity of Christ's saving work, which brings with it the rise of the Church as his minister and instrument, [which was] clearly manifested in Assisi, despite the differences of religious professions that were by no means hidden or attenuated), differences of every sort, and first of all religious differences, insofar as they are reductive of God's plan, prove to belong to another order.
>
> Whereas the order of unity is the one that goes back to creation and redemption and is therefore, in this sense, "divine", these differences and divergences, even religious ones, can be traced back instead to a "human act" and must be overcome in our progress toward the realization of the grandiose plan of unity that presides over creation. There are, of course, differences that reflect the genius and the spiritual "riches" given by God to the nations (cf. *Ad gentes* 11). I am not referring to these. I mean to allude to the differences that manifest the limits, the developments, and the falls of the human spirit ensnared by the spirit of evil in history (*Lumen gentium* 16).[2]

If Africa today is the lung of the Church, the Church for her part is Africa's opportunity. Only an African family converted to the plan of God—who wants it to be through the sacrament of matrimony a sign of his Love manifested in Jesus Christ—can ultimately resist the new colonization that threatens it today.

For the Church, the Family of God in Africa, therefore, it is a question of giving to the world the fruit expected from the tree of the ecclesiological option "Church, the Family of God" made by the 1994 synod. We must never cease to devise strategies to this effect.

From the challenge to the strategy of evangelization

In the same Africa where *Islam and Christianity* share the space and the dynamic forces of the continent, the encounter between Catholics and

---

[2] Address of John Paul II to the Roman Curia at the Exchange of Christmas Greetings (December 22, 1986), 5 (translated from Italian).

Muslims is inevitable in some countries like Senegal, and these may lead individuals to consider interfaith marriage. This is a reality that should be taken into account with the requisite *pastoral prudence*, of course, but also with the demand for the *evangelizing mission* of the family.

To illustrate this statement, let us examine the case of Senegal, in which the Muslims are in the great majority (90 to 92 percent) and the Catholics a small minority (5 to 6 percent).

"When I reach the age to marry, I will marry a Catholic girl!" This was one of the precious hopes cherished by a young Senegalese Muslim, who did in fact marry a Catholic woman. This case reflects many others. Indeed, in this country there are many Muslims who praise the qualities that they observe in Christian women: their seriousness, delicacy, and tenderness, their honesty and neatness in housekeeping, and so on. And so there is no lack of requests for a dispensation for disparity of cult on the desks of the bishops.

Although mixed marriages, which are much less numerous because of the small percentage of other Christians (between 1 and 2 percent), pose no great difficulties, it must be acknowledged that marriages between Christians and Muslims raise more than one question: Should they be accepted, discouraged, rejected? The answers are different, depending on one's convictions.

Some think that this form of marriage is an opportunity for dialogue between Christians and Muslims and that it can strengthen that dialogue. Indeed, given the number of Senegalese families with both Muslim and Catholic members, it must be acknowledged that the family is actually a major place and setting for the Islamo-Christian dialogue. This is cause for rejoicing, and we must take care to develop better pastoral care to the family that more fully incorporates this fact, thus contributing to the victory of love over the barriers of religious differences.

Nevertheless, there are many real difficulties. We should mention the different views of marriage. While the Christian is formed to contract and live a monogamous, indissoluble marriage, the Muslim grows up thinking that a marriage can involve polygamy and end in divorce. Even if the Muslim party accepts the Christian view at the start, married life and its difficulties may bring about changes of opinion and, therefore, conflicts between spouses.

The dangers of apostasy by the Catholic party, especially women, are real, too, and quite a few cases occur. The pressure from one's milieu,

especially from the family of the Muslim spouse, the personal development of the latter, the saying that is heard unceasingly, that "the wife
has no religion; she adheres to her husband's", and other reasons get the
better of the Catholic party's determination to keep her Christian faith.

Other difficulties include the education of the children in views of
life that are different in some regards, the choice of a religion for them
during their childhood or as they reach adulthood, whether to give them
religious instruction or to postpone it, and other questions....

In short, marriages between Christians and Muslims in Senegal offer
opportunities for Islamo-Christian dialogue but involve serious difficulties for the common life of the spouses and dangers for the faith.

In conclusion, let us simply open up the two fields of ecumenism and
interreligious dialogue, in which Christ's lay faithful are called to devise
missionary strategies in their mixed and interfaith marriages; an analysis
of the environment can discern the opportunities to be seized and the
dangers to be forestalled.

Strategy of interreligious dialogue. Experience has taught us sufficiently,
particularly in Senegal, that one should not make plans for marriage
between Christians and Muslims without adequate knowledge about
marriage according to Islam and about the possibilities offered by the
national legislation concerning the family, for example that of Senegal.

Thus to ignore the *options for polygamy* that Senegalese family law
offers to every citizen of Senegal, including Catholics, would be to commit oneself blindly to a path in which the meaning of Christian marriage
would not be acknowledged by one's spouse. Catechesis and marriage
preparation must therefore include the possibility of marriage with a
dispensation for disparity of cult, not as something inevitable, but as
a historic situation in which the Church is called to proclaim the Love of
God for every human being, as manifested in Jesus Christ.

Hence the Church, the Family of God in Africa, is obliged to analyze
constantly the paths of life on which Catholics, Muslims, and the faithful
of traditional African religions walk together, so as to avoid granting
dispensations for disparity of cult that lead their beneficiaries into an
impasse because the risks caused by the obstacles and real difficulties
were insufficiently taken into account.

However, marriage contracted with a dispensation for disparity
of cult can also and even must, in the case of the Catholic party, be considered from the perspective of *interreligious dialogue* in all the forms

thereof recognized by the Magisterium, in the teaching of Vatican II (see *Nostra aetate*, 3), as developed in the Magisterial teaching of Saint John Paul II, and as put into practice by the Pontifical Council for Inter-religious Dialogue.

> The Catholic Church rejects nothing that is true and holy in these religions. She regards with sincere reverence those ways of conduct and of life, those precepts and teachings which, though differing in many aspects from the ones she holds and sets forth, nonetheless often reflect a ray of that Truth which enlightens all men. Indeed, she proclaims, and ever must proclaim Christ "the way, the truth, and the life" (John 14:6), in whom men may find the fullness of religious life, in whom God has reconciled all things to Himself.
>
> The Church, therefore, exhorts her sons, that through dialogue and collaboration with the followers of other religions, carried out with prudence and love and in witness to the Christian faith and life, they recognize, preserve, and promote the good things, spiritual and moral, as well as the socio-cultural values found among these men. (*Nostra aetate* 2)

The second strategy will be the *strategy of ecumenical dialogue*, for which Vatican II also gives us the essential outline in the decree *Ad gentes*:

> Insofar as religious conditions allow, ecumenical activity should be furthered in such a way that, excluding any appearance of indifference or confusion on the one hand, or of unhealthy rivalry on the other, Catholics should cooperate in a brotherly spirit with their separated brethren, according to the norms of the Decree on Ecumenism, making before the nations a common profession of faith, insofar as their beliefs are common, in God and in Jesus Christ, and cooperating in social and in technical projects as well as in cultural and religious ones. (*Ad gentes* 15)

In today's Africa, where the variety of Christian communities and sects of Christian or African origin inevitably creates confusion that seriously endangers the faith of the Catholic party who is living in a *mixed marriage*, the lay faithful and their pastors must develop a pastoral program of preparation for such marriages, one that is based on a precise knowledge of the denominations that call themselves Christian. Catechesis in Africa must include this dimension (cf. decree *Ad gentes* 15, paragraph 5), with a view to a Church-Family of God that is faithful to the conciliar decree *Unitatis redintegratio* on ecumenism and in keeping with the option of the 1994 Synod for Africa.

Initial information should be given about the relative closeness among the Christian denominations. Even though this closeness (or division, to look at things from the less fortunate side) is not a matter of African origin, it inevitably affects our Churches that resulted from missionary efforts and the Afro-Christian Churches or communities. Baptized Africans, who in many respects are still neophytes, can and must strive to experience the closeness between Christians as disciples who learn together to know, love, and serve better their Teacher, Jesus Christ. Families resulting from mixed marriages are places and environments of ecumenism. May they work to promote it, despite the difficulties!

The same goes for families resulting from disparate marriages. They are places and environments of interreligious dialogue. May they work to promote it, despite the difficulties and the stumbling blocks!

3. The Challenge of Dispensation and Permission

The challenge of the dispensation that is to be requested and granted for disparate marriages, or of permission in the case of mixed marriages, proves to be an exercise in *pastoral prudence* that is all the more difficult, given its capital importance for the future. It is necessary to have taken into account the whole dimension of pastoral prudence in order to face the challenge of requesting and granting a dispensation.

It is necessary to understand that the challenge does not face the local Ordinary alone who is responsible for granting a dispensation. It faces, first of all, the person who requests the dispensation and his family, then the pastor who must forward a well-founded request to the Ordinary, and finally the one who ultimately decides the matter. All of these persons have the duty to perform an act of prudence with regard to the request and granting of a dispensation.

Meeting the challenge of a request for dispensation or permission begins, therefore, with an in-depth catechesis about the mystery of the person and communal encounter of baptized persons with Jesus Christ, in all departments of their life, including marital and family life. Meeting this challenge of dispensation presupposes also a catechesis on marriage that makes very clear its *sacramental character* and its dimension as a *vocation* and a divine mission, and not as a merely social obligation or necessity that makes celibacy seem to be a failure. Indeed, it is not uncommon to meet women who feel obliged to marry, of course to avoid loneliness, but also in order to enjoy the respect and special treatment that society gives to married women or even for economic security. Then the desire to marry, at all costs, may stifle any other concern and lead to apostasy.

While not acknowledging that a husband has the power to repudiate his wife (or a wife her husband) for any reason whatsoever (see Mt 19:6), Jesus Christ also rejects the logic of the apostles, who thought that, if such was the case "it is not expedient to marry" (see Mt 19:10). Is not a desire to marry at any cost, in any circumstances whatsoever, the result of a will for power or, conversely, of resignation when faced with the serious demands of the faith or merely the serious demands of living? "For there are eunuchs who have been so from birth, and there are eunuchs who have been made eunuchs by men, and there are eunuchs who have made themselves eunuchs for the sake of the kingdom of heaven" (Mt 19:12).

The challenge of requesting a dispensation or a permission is therefore a real challenge facing the member of Christ's lay faithful, particularly to his virtue of prudence and his fidelity to Christ: to follow him to the end, by analyzing and avoiding risks of denying him; preferring to lose a certain potential spouse rather than to abandon Jesus Christ. Thus prudence does not merely consist in not doing something. Although it is about gauging the negative consequences of the act that one is about to perform, so as to avoid them, it is also about gauging the commitments that result from the acts that one performs, with their positive implications that should be promoted.

In order to meet the challenge of requesting a dispensation or permission, it is necessary to have authentically Christian families, families that have been evangelized in the way described in *Evangelii nuntiandi* 18 and 19; families capable of helping all their members to analyze the risks of losing their Catholic faith; capable of helping them to make a prudent commitment to live out that same faith in an interfaith or mixed marriage.

Do lay Catholic faithful whose circumstances in life lead them to ask for a dispensation from the requirement to marry a Catholic in order to start a Christian family supported by the sacrament of matrimony come from a truly evangelized African family? Do not a large number of requests for dispensation mean an even greater need to evangelize the family and its members?

As long as our African families are not profoundly Christian, the challenge of dispensation or permission will arise constantly, and it will always be accompanied by the challenge of a true ecumenical dialogue, in the case of a mixed marriage, and by the challenge of a true interreligious dialogue, in the case of interfaith marriage with a dispensation for disparity of cult. What pastoral approach should be promoted? What pastoral plan should be promoted then, not only to preserve the faith of Catholics in mixed marriages and in interfaith marriages, but furthermore so that they might be missionaries in their everyday living condition?

The complexity of the challenge posed by mixed and interfaith marriages therefore must not elude pastors or the Catholic lay faithful. The initial challenge posed by mixed marriage and disparate marriage for the Catholic lay faithful and their pastors is the *appreciation* of the plan for such marriage and the appreciation of the consequences of such marriages. The pastors and lay faithful who address the questions of dispensation cannot spare themselves the effort of a moral reflection on this subject, any more than the Ordinary who must give this dispensation.

The priest who forwards a request for a dispensation or for permission to the Ordinary must therefore show evidence of a "practical knowledge of the situation, of sagacity, and of discernment" of the obstacles to be avoided, certainly, but also of the opportunities to be seized. In other words, the step of *internal analysis of strengths and weaknesses* of the circumstances and persons and the step of *external analysis of the opportunities and threats* of their environment have to become a regular pastoral habit.

This twofold analysis is not too much when what is at stake is the celebration of a marriage, the symbol of God's unfailing fidelity toward man, the mutual fidelity of the spouses, and their faithfulness to God. It is not too much, either, when we remember that marriage is the foundation of the Christian family, the domestic church, the source of vocations to marriage as well as to the priestly and religious life.

Meeting the challenge of requesting and granting dispensation or permission requires also that we listen to Scripture, as Jean-Louis Bruguès, O.P., a member of the International Theological Commission, recommends:

> In the Old Testament, the Wisdom literature taught that prudence required certain qualities of mind that were necessary in order for a human being to live well: docility, observance of the Law, justice. The prudent

man was a clever and pious man who counted essentially on God's help in order to lead a happy life. Be prudent as serpents and innocent as doves, Jesus recommended (Mt 10:16). Elsewhere, he held up as an example the wise steward to whom the Master entrusted his goods (Lk 12:42–43). We easily understand why moral exhortation is accompanied by the praise of knowledge and why some intellectual qualities are necessary in order to enter into the Kingdom (Mt 25:1–13).

The author enriches his reflection by citing one by a colleague of his: "Prudence", writes Marie-Dominique Chenu, "is precisely the endowment through which my reason, true to itself, is able to govern the vast changeableness of my behavior and to refract into my most difficult actions eternal divine attributes of Truth, Justice, and authentic fulfillment."[3]

The Church in Africa, therefore, cannot minimize, much less ignore, the challenge of requesting and granting dispensation or permission. This demand cannot be reduced to an effort to discourage mixed or interfaith marriages. It is a question of acting prudently and not of a fearful attitude that inhibits apostles. Above all and first of all, it is a matter of living the faith in Jesus Christ. It is a matter of firmly believing that he comes to us in the situations and events of our lives, as his appearances after his Resurrection teach us. It is about the desire to encounter him as did the apostles, the Samaritan woman, Zacchaeus, Saul who later became Saint Paul, and many other saints: to encounter him so that he might transform us.

It is also a question of hearing him call us by name and sending us to be his witnesses (Acts 1:8), to proclaim the Good News of salvation by our deeds and our words (Lk 9:1–6; 10:1–3). In short, it is a matter of expending continual efforts to live as disciples and faithful witnesses of Jesus Christ in the marital and familial community, whether with a baptized non-Catholic or with a non-Christian believer.

Conclusion

Part of the mission of the Church in Africa is to deepen the theological and pastoral reflection on *mixed and disparate marriages*, to develop everywhere fruitful pastoral approaches for accompanying Catholics

---

[3] Marie-Dominique Chenu, *Aquinas and His Role in Theology*, trans. Paul Philibert (Collegeville, Minn.: Liturgical Press, 2002), 110.

who wish to enter into such marriages as well as the young men and women involved in the resulting families. This is therefore a *major challenge*, in addition to others, that calls for the attention and solicitude of the Church, the Family of God, in all situations and problems of the family in Africa, so that, saved by Christ, it might be the mold in which is formed an Africa that is renewed according to the plan of God, Father, Son, and Holy Spirit.

Pastoral Care to Wounded Families

Archbishop Samuel Kleda

Introduction

How can we assist spiritually the ever greater number of families who are wounded because of the crisis of marriage and the family that our society is experiencing? This is a big and urgent problem that the Church faces today in the context of her pastoral care to the family. The Church tries to open her doors to all her children, because by her nature she is a mother and she is the sacrament of salvation, according to the Lord's will. But to what point can the Church become involved in welcoming wounded families, spouses who are divorced and have each contracted a second marriage? What place can they have within the Christian community?

In fact, there are many persons who live in distressing situations that arose within the family. There are multiple and varied causes for them. The pastor of souls finds himself confronted every day with all these situations. He is called to welcome and accompany all these persons so as to bring them comfort, consolation, love, and peace, like the apostles who traveled about the villages of Galilee (cf. Mt 12–13). In this commitment, the pastor must also take as his point of departure Jesus, who is the first Missionary.

The better to address all these problems, we will first take a look at the crisis situation that today's families are experiencing, before presenting the appropriate doctrinal and pastoral solutions that the Church promotes.

Archbishop Samuel Kleda is archbishop of Douala.

1. Family Situations Today

A. The crisis of family life

For half a century, the family has undergone great upheavals, which have undermined the basis of the traditional family, the basic cell that welcomes a human being into the world. The values that made the family what it really is are disputed and rejected. New ideologies have appeared and have made it their business to invent new forms of family. Throughout the world, no family is immune to these changes, these mutations that are becoming imperative, because the whole world has gradually become involved in a movement of irreversible transformation. This transformation has been due, since the Second World War, to the industrialization of the world, which is in transition from farm life to an industrial civilization. A consumer economy has gradually made headway.

The entrance of the communications media into the family, particularly television, manages to upset it. Television presents new life-styles, which fascinate everyone, and they gain total acceptance. These new models completely overturn family life. Family members spend most of their time in front of the television screen, and that modifies their habits: little by little, conversation within families disappears; members of the same family no longer have the time to talk to one another. Television goes so far as to play with the art of living: people consume what they see onscreen. A new way of being has now set up shop. Studying Italian society, Sabino Acquaviva neatly sums up in these words the changes that our societies are undergoing: "Everything is changing: our way of speaking, loving, spontaneously situating ourselves in society, our way of making friendships and living with others: also changing is our attitude toward life, toward its meaning as well as toward the meaning of death, toward politics. In short, our way of living and thinking is being transformed, just like the framework of cultural reference."[1]

African societies are not spared these upheavals. Changes have been noted especially since 1960, the date when most African countries gained independence. These political demands shape different personalities. New ways of life appear as a result of contact with everything that

---

[1] Sabino Acquaviva, "Comportement sexuel et mutation sociale dans une société en transition, le cas italien", in *Concilium* 193 (1984): 46.

comes from elsewhere, especially from the countries of the Northern Hemisphere; instruction in schools affects almost all societies. The title of a novel by the Nigerian writer Chinua Achebe is quite revealing on this subject: *Things Fall Apart*.[2] The author lets us watch the collapse of traditional values, which African societies try to preserve, but in vain. African families find themselves confronted by these changes and do not resist their influence; they break down and vainly try to find other new paths by which to flourish. Unfortunately, they can take only what they receive.

In this context, a new concept of sexuality arose. People talk about the "sexual revolution".[3] One notes, indeed, a reaction against the Christian concept of sexuality that is insinuating itself into the family: sexuality is quite simply reified and trivialized; it even becomes a commodity. In this realm of sexuality, there are no more limits: homosexuality is proclaimed today; persons with homosexual tendencies publicly display their choice and want to be recognized as such. Some go so far as to speak about marriage between persons of the same sex. At the recent Extraordinary Synod of Bishops in October 2014, in Rome, the Synod Fathers clearly stated that never in the history of the Church were homosexual unions considered to be marriage.[4] And this is the complex situation in which the disciples of Jesus Christ are living; they have to be his witnesses within it.

B. *These wounded families*

"Wounded families" should be understood to mean, above all: separated persons, divorced persons who have not remarried, the divorced and remarried, as well as single-parent families (abandoned persons). But there are many other causes of suffering in families, especially in Africa.

These wounds, which cast so many families into despair, as we have just observed, result from the upheaval and transformation that our society is undergoing today. It must be noted that our era has witnessed the largest number of divorces in history.[5] Spouses who have experienced

---

[2] Chinua Achebe, *Things Fall Apart* (Nigeria, 1958; reprinted, New York: Anchor, 1994).

[3] Gregory Baum and John Coleman, editorial in *Concilium* 193 (1984): 7–11.

[4] Synod of Bishops, XIV Extraordinary General Assembly, *Lineamenta* (Vatican City, 2014), no. 55.

[5] See J. Gaudemet, *Le mariage en Occident: Les moeurs et le droit* (Paris: Cerf, 1987), 12–14.

the failure of their marital union carry that failure with them for the rest of their lives, even if they succeed in rebuilding another home. We might mention, among others, the suffering of those who unjustly undergo separation, divorce, or abandonment; the torment of those who have been compelled to break up their common life because of mistreatment by their spouse; the bitterness of these single parents who have to bear alone the responsibility for the family's household, the upbringing of the children, and so on.

In Africa, a home without a child is considered a failure; this is a problem we find in Sacred Scripture: the suffering of the future mother of Samuel drives her to the temple to beg the Lord to give her a boy (see 1 Sam 1:9–18); also the distress of Zechariah and Elizabeth, whose prayers the Lord answered by giving them a child (see Lk 1:5–25). In African societies, spouses who find themselves in this situation will do anything to have a child. The wife alone is often accused of sterility, and she is dismissed from the home, even if Christian marriage was celebrated. Another solution is often considered: the husband takes another wife. The family thus ends up in a situation of polygamy, and there you have a family that will never again experience true peace.

There are families in which one of the spouses falls seriously ill or becomes disabled. The spouses sometimes separate; if the wife is the one who is sick, she is sent back to live with her parents, and they now have to take care of their daughter. The husband starts life over with another woman. Similarly, there are families in which one of the spouses is an alcoholic or drug addict or has joined a sect that imposes on the couple a different life-style that disrupts marital life.

Among the causes of suffering within families there are also infidelity, violence, and lying. There is another phenomenon that affects more and more families: incest. Many children are the victims of it.

Moreover, there are families in which the spouses are separated for other reasons: war, prison, work. Many families find themselves in this situation in Africa because of the increasing number of hotbeds of tension and war.

Today, in Africa, material poverty is becoming one of the most serious causes of suffering for many families. This phenomenon, unfortunately, is only growing. For couples living in a town, there is often unemployment. Entire families find themselves without work, without lodging, without the minimum needed to survive, living in abject poverty, incapable of bringing up their children. It is difficult for the members of these families to thrive spiritually.

One last form of suffering that can be observed involves couples who are not well prepared for marriage, who have not understood the meaning of family life and have not agreed to give themselves totally to each other. Their life as a couple is spent in misunderstanding and disagreement. These are couples who will never know the beauty of family life; they are married, and they live together, but they do not form a true family.

All this suggests the crisis that the family is experiencing today. All the families in the world are affected by it. Given this crisis, the Church has to proclaim to families the Good News, the Good News of life, peace, and love. She must listen to each family with love, respect, and discernment.

2. Pastoral and Doctrinal Solutions with Regard to Wounded Families

A. Jesus, manifestation of God's mercy to mankind

In dealing with afflicted persons, Jesus Christ was always full of compassion, giving them the necessary attention and performing acts to relieve their pain. He never closed his heart to any human being. Everyone who came to him found compassion and comfort; he himself also took the initiative to go out to people who were suffering, helpless persons who had no recourse. Here are a few examples of this manifestation of love: Jesus is in a desert place, and a large crowd sets out to look for him (cf. Mt 14:13–21). In that desert place, Jesus finds himself confronted by that crowd. He has pity on them. Not only does he heal the sick among them, but he feeds that hungry crowd by performing a miracle; he does not leave that crowd to fend for itself, and thus, as the Messiah, he shows them God's goodness.

Jesus comes to the aid of single persons who are struck by misfortune or are accused. In Luke 7:11–17, a widow loses her only son. We can well imagine the suffering of that woman from Nain. As they are getting ready to bury the child, Jesus consoles the woman by reviving her son. In Luke 8:40–56, at the explicit request of the head of a synagogue, Jesus heals his only daughter, who was on the point of death. A woman who for a long time was suffering from a hemorrhage touches Jesus and regains her health (see Mk 5:25–34). The evangelist Mark accurately notes the suffering of that woman: "And there was a woman who had had a flow of blood for twelve years, and who had suffered much under many physicians, and had spent all that she had, and was no better but rather grew worse" (vv. 25–26). In the presence of Jesus, hope is reborn for that woman. She rediscovers joy in living. In Luke 9:37–43, a man begs Jesus to deliver his son from an evil spirit that makes him suffer greatly. This man presents to Jesus his suffering, the distress of his whole family. Jesus delivers his child from the evil spirit. All of these afflicted persons, therefore, who suffer because of their illness or because of the infirmity of their close relatives, find in Jesus consolation and peace through his answer to their prayers.

In his determination to liberate everyone, Jesus comes into contact with persons whom society regards as sinners and shuns. Jesus and his disciples have a meal at the house of a chief tax collector, Zacchaeus, despite the criticism of the Pharisees who are partaking of the meal with them. Zacchaeus' heart had been touched by Jesus' presence. The tax collector stands up in front of the guests and publicly confesses his sinful state. He resolves to give up his former life: he decides to distribute half of his possessions and to stop stealing. Zacchaeus converts because the Lord went to stay at his house; he showed him God's mercy. Jesus, acting in his Father's name, does not condemn the sinner, but rather his welcoming attitude invites the sinner to change his ways. A woman was caught in the very act of adultery. She is led into the presence of Jesus by the scribes and Pharisees, who demand that she be stoned, as the law requires (cf. Jn 8:1–11). Yet Jesus does not condemn her; rather, he invites her to change her life: "Neither do I condemn you; go, and do not sin again" (v. 11). Jesus asks this adulterous woman to look toward the future, to lead her life in a new way, according to God's plan. In order to do that, conversion is necessary, and this is what the tax collector Zacchaeus resolved to do in his life, too.

Our Lord's attitude toward these sick, suffering, and wounded persons is explained and summed up in these tender words that he spoke after eating with publicans and sinners: "Those who are well have no need of a physician, but those who are sick. Go and learn what this means, 'I desire mercy, and not sacrifice.' For I came not to call the righteous, but sinners" (Mt 9:12–13). Our Lord, by everything he did, showed that he had come for persons who are suffering, who are abandoned and rejected by society. He did not side with the Pharisees and scribes who thought they were just and condemned other people (cf. Lk 18:10–12). He placed himself at the service of all those poor people who are marginalized or rejected by society. He welcomed sinners, and this was noticed by the Pharisees and scribes (cf. Lk 15:2). He is for the world the true face of God, his merciful face. This is why the author of the Letter to the Hebrews calls Jesus the "merciful and faithful high priest" (Heb 2:17). He plays this role in mankind's relations with God.

This is what Christ Jesus is for men, for those who suffer or are desperate. With him, the pain of everyone is relieved, because everyone encounters his gentle, lowly heart (cf. Mt 11:29); in his presence, everyone rediscovers hope and the joy of living. With him, everyone rediscovers his dignity. When the sinner becomes open to God's mercy, he is reborn to new life. Consequently, the pastoral care of wounded families requires above all an attitude of mercy, like that of Jesus.

B. The pastor following Christ at the service of the family

Every pastor, imitating Christ, his sole model, should show to the faithful who are entrusted to his pastoral care, especially to those who are afflicted, the love, kindness, and tenderness of God. He must have toward them an attitude of compassion as Christ did and be ready to lay down his life for them. The apostle Saint Paul gives witness to this gift of self to the faithful of Thessalonica, a community that he founded and to which he addressed his first letters. Since he had not been able to complete the formation of these Christian faithful, he continued this work by writing two letters to them. Here is how the apostle expressed his love for the children whom he had engendered in Jesus: "We were gentle among you, like a nurse taking care of her children. So, being affectionately desirous of you, we were ready to share with you not only the gospel of God but also our own selves, because you had become very dear to us" (1 Thess 2:7–8). This love must be expressed through the pastor's generosity and availability. The faithful should encounter in him the face of Jesus Christ, the heart of Jesus Christ. In the most difficult cases involving couples, for which no doctrinal solution is possible, the pastor must exhaust all the possibilities and be able to offer relief and comfort to the afflicted couples. He must see in the faces of each couple experiencing difficulty the face of the suffering Christ, who tells us:

"Truly, I say to you, as you did it to one of the least of these my brethren, you did it to me" (Mt 25:40).

In the current crisis that the family is experiencing, the pastor of souls has to adopt an attitude that brings him closer to couples who are experiencing difficulties. For him, it is a matter of showing great, boundless generosity, welcoming all the faithful with respect and love, helping the poor and always being compassionate toward all who are living in difficult situations. In this connection, Saint Ambrose, that great shepherd of souls, proved to have limitless generosity, opening his heart to everyone who came to him, especially the poor, and showing compassion to sinners. Here is what he wrote to Auxentius: "If the emperor asked me for all of my belongings, my lands, my money, I would make no objection, although all my property belongs to the poor. But divine things are by no means subject to the emperor."[6] Here is an example of a pastor who lives for the poor and has no personal belongings. The pastor of Milan was very sensitive to persons who were suffering, to the point of truly suffering with them. "Every time the sin of a guilty person is revealed to me, may I be able to take part in his sorrow. Instead of rebuking him haughtily, may I be able to grieve and weep."[7] Saint Ambrose shows us that a pastor must be very close to his faithful and share deeply in their sufferings.

As for Saint Augustine, he shows us the example of a pastor's true love for his faithful, following the example of Jesus Christ. We find in him a concern about leading the whole person to Jesus Christ: "Let us fear more lest the spark of life in the living stones [of the Church] be quenched through our absence, than lest the stones and timbers of our earthly buildings be burned in our presence. Let us fear more lest the members of Christ's body should die for want of spiritual food, than lest the members of our own bodies, being overpowered by the violence of enemies, should be racked with torture."[8] Saint Augustine nicely expresses our Lord's desire not to lose one single person (cf. Mt 18:14). This should also be the concern of every pastor of souls. For the pastor, this is about going to meet wounded families who are waiting to be comforted.

Therefore, we are invited today to review our strategy as a pastor. There is an urgent need for new pastoral approaches. We have to

---

[6] Quoted by Sister Gabriel Peters, in *Lire les Pères de l'Église* (Paris: Cerf, 1981), 653.

[7] Quoted by Sister Gabriel Peters, ibid., 660.

[8] Quoted by Sister Gabriel Peters, ibid., 733.

open our chanceries and rectories to everyone and, above all, dispel the myth that the pastor should not be easily accessible. We have to break through the bureaucracy that we often set up, which distances us from the people. The pastor is above all a man of the people and for the people. The faithful have the right to "bother" those whom the Church places at their service (cf. Mt 15:23–28). We must be animated by our Master's desire to go everywhere proclaiming the Good News (cf. Lk 10:1). Animated by the concern to meet all the faithful—that is how we should be in the Lord's service. Saint Paul expressed this concern well as he performed his ministry: "There is the daily pressure upon me of my anxiety for all the churches. Who is weak, and I am not weak? Who is made to fall, and I am not indignant?" (2 Cor 11:28–29). Therefore we must be converted, so that we can be open to the pastoral challenges that families encounter today.

C. The primordial role of the Christian community

We cannot forget the role that the Christian community is called to play in the context of accompanying wounded couples and families. When a Christian community takes charge of watching over each one of its members, it is exemplifying a true spirit of love and sharing. Think, for instance, of the beautiful witness of parish communities whose members form a true family, communities that live according to the Gospel spirit, which one recognizes as a Church Family—an expression confirmed by Saint John Paul II in *Ecclesia in Africa*.

These Living Ecclesial Communities (French acronym CEV, from *Communautés Ecclésiales Vivantes*) were described in *Ecclesia in Africa* in these terms: "Primarily they should be places engaged in evangelizing themselves, so that subsequently they can bring the Good News to others; they should moreover be communities which pray and listen to God's Word, encourage the members themselves to take on responsibility, learn to live an ecclesial life, and reflect on different human problems in the light of the Gospel."[9]

Indeed, when all the members of a living ecclesial community care for one another, they suffer to see a member in difficult straits. Couples who have more experience accompany weaker young couples. All the members of the community should live according to the invaluable

---

[9] John Paul II, *Ecclesia in Africa* (1995), 89.

advice of Saint Paul: "If one member suffers, all suffer together; if one member is honored, all rejoice together" (1 Cor 12:26). This goes well with the duty performed by the traditional African community. Accompanying a family so that it discovers its mission is everyone's business.

D. The need to develop a good pastoral program for marriage and the family

Every pastor is conscious of the mission he has received from Jesus to proclaim the Gospel. More than ever, today he has to confront the crisis that is shaking and destabilizing families. In order to do so, he needs a tool on which to rely: a well-developed pastoral plan. The pastor's task will be, not just to strive to solve problems, but rather to set in place basic elements for the formation of families according to God's plan. This will allow him to avoid many of the disastrous situations we know so well today. Within the framework of this essay, it is not possible to develop a detailed pastoral plan. Nevertheless, I am anxious to describe the different stages that should be taken into account.

The first stage of marriage preparation consists of a remote preparation, which is provided within the family. All the education that a child receives within the family prepares him to start a family later. In Africa, the first duty that parents have toward their children is to help them start a family. Similar cases can be found in the Bible: let us mention Abraham, who has the duty to provide for his son Isaac a wife from his own clan. He entrusts this task to his servant and makes him swear so as to make sure he will carry out his wishes (see Gen 24:1–4). This education is provided above all by the living witness of the parents. The children, seeing their parents love one another, are happy to live in peace within the family and discover the beauty of family life. Then they discover the real meaning of true family life.

The second stage is engagement, which should be promoted today. During this stage, the young person chooses someone with whom he will live for the rest of his life. It is therefore good to help the young person to make a responsible choice. When the two young people have met, they begin then to associate with one another. This time of engagement allows them to get to know each other so that they can live their whole life together. Since in African societies marriage involves the two communities from which the two young people come, they accompany the two young people in the actualization of their plan. During the engagement period, the two communities get to know one another, too. An investigation is carried out by each of the communities so as to know the other party. The involvement of each community gives it the chance to intervene later to help the couple if there are difficulties. As for the Christian community, it has a major role to play: accompanying these young people who are seeking to start a family by giving them a Christian formation. In some particular Churches, centers of formation have been established, which are called "the school of engaged couples". Thus it is up to each episcopal conference to set up structures to help the young couples (canon 1062, §1). An engagement helps the young people to begin their common life on their wedding day.

The third stage of immediate preparation crowns the preceding stages: it prepares the future spouses to celebrate their conjugal union. It must have a well-developed program, with a clearly determined duration, as Saint John Paul II recommended. The episcopal conferences and the pastors "will also take steps to see that there is issued a Directory for the Pastoral Care of the Family. In this they should lay down, in the first place, the minimum content, duration, and method of the 'Preparation Courses,' balancing the different aspects—doctrinal, pedagogical, legal, and medical—concerning marriage, and structuring them in such a way that those preparing for marriage will not only receive an intellectual training but will also feel a desire to enter actively into the ecclesial community."[10] Anything concerning marriage and capable of helping the spouses should be the subject matter of the formation of future married couples. A good catechesis must be offered to them. No couple should be blessed unless they have received formation. This important stage will enable them to discover the beauty of marriage and the values of family life according to God's plan. Nowadays it is good to understand that the family is a divine institution and that starting a family is a vocation for the husband as well as for the wife. In being joined by the bond of marriage, the spouses enter into God's plan.

The basis of this formation must consist of biblical texts. This will help the spouses to welcome family life, which is made up of joys and of sufferings, too. Every pastor must understand the need to prepare future spouses well for marriage. This preparation is necessary in order to achieve strong, stable marriages that are capable of withstanding all sorts of difficulties.

---

[10]John Paul II, *Familiaris consortio* (1986) (*FS*), 66.

The fourth stage or the last point that should be understood and on which we ought to insist is post-matrimonial accompaniment. There is a tendency to think that after the wedding ceremony one's service to the young married couple has been completed. But after the wedding, the couple's life together begins, with all its joys and sufferings, when the spouses find themselves face to face. This is when misunderstandings arise that can easily lead to divorce. This is when we ought to be close to them. In the major African cities, when young couples are going through difficult times, they are on their own, far from their parents, far from the village communities. Lacking experience in married life, they insist more on their disagreements than on what unites them, like the couple in the story told by the French author François Mauriac in his novel *Viper's Tangle*.[11] The fictional couple wasted away in failure, like so many couples we know.

This is when couples who have a good deal of life experience should come to the aid of young couples who are having difficulty. The pastor should organize this very important accompaniment. This post-matrimonial accompaniment can help many young couples start a true family according to God's plan. All the stages just enumerated deserve the utmost attention of pastors to whom souls have been entrusted.

E. Responses to some wounded families

The messenger of the Good News, the pastor, is faced with all the difficult and complex situations that families are experiencing, situations to which he has to respond so as to relieve, console, and comfort these afflicted persons in the name of Jesus, whose merciful heart is open to all. Every person, whatever his desperate situation, finds welcome with him; this constant attention is given today by the Church. God manifested his will to save every person (cf. 1 Tim 2:4). Thus no one should feel excluded from God's plan. This, indeed, is the sense in which every wounded person can turn to Jesus.

The situation of divorced and remarried couples is a matter of particular concern for every pastor. As baptized persons, they belong to the Church and are children of the Church. Nevertheless, they are not in complete communion with her, since they cannot celebrate their

---

[11] François Mauriac, *Le noeud de vipères* (Paris: Bernard Grasset, 1933); trans. Gerard Hopkins as *Viper's Tangle* (Chicago: Loyola Press, 2005).

marriage in the Church because of an impediment due to a previous marital union of one or both spouses.

Therefore, they cannot receive the Eucharist, the Body of Christ, or the sacrament of penance. Since Vatican Council II, this issue has preoccupied the Church, for the rate of legally and sacramentally married couples who later separate is very high, especially in the highly industrialized countries. The literature on this subject is quite extensive, and the opinions of theologians and of other thinkers diverge widely. The Catholic Church, however, remains faithful to the teaching of her Master, who made marriage between a man and a woman a sacrament. A validly celebrated marriage is indissoluble. Here is the answer given by our Lord to the Pharisees who had asked him about the possibility of a husband repudiating his wife:

"From the beginning of creation, God made them male and female. For this reason a man shall leave his father and mother and be joined to his wife, and the two shall become one flesh. So they are no longer two but one flesh. What therefore God has joined together, let not man put asunder."

And in the house the disciples asked him again about this matter. And he said to them, "Whoever divorces his wife and marries another, commits adultery against her; and if she divorces her husband and marries another, she commits adultery." (Mk 10:6–12)

This is the Church's position, which Saint John Paul II clearly set forth. It is helpful to read what the saintly pope wrote:

However, the Church reaffirms her practice, which is based upon Sacred Scripture, of not admitting to Eucharistic Communion divorced persons who have remarried. They are unable to be admitted thereto from the fact that their state and condition of life objectively contradict that union of love between Christ and the Church which is signified and effected by the Eucharist. Besides this, there is another special pastoral reason: if these people were admitted to the Eucharist, the faithful would be led into error and confusion regarding the Church's teaching about the indissolubility of marriage.[12]

Pope Benedict XVI, then Cardinal Joseph Ratzinger, offered a good explanation of this position by reviewing each point in this passage by

---

[12] FC 84.

Saint John Paul II, in a document issued by the Congregation for the Doctrine of the Faith.[13] The XIV Extraordinary General Assembly of the Synod of Bishops in October 2014 once again reaffirmed the indissolubility of marriage.[14] For the Church, this is a matter of remaining faithful to the teaching of our Lord Jesus Christ.

Nevertheless, the Church does show to all who are wounded the mercy of God, his love for every person, in the sense that he rejects no one. All possible doctrinal and pastoral solutions must be utilized by the Church in order to be close to those who are suffering in the context of marriage and the family. Saint John Paul II neatly described the place and the welcome that should be given to the divorced and remarried:

> They should be encouraged to listen to the word of God, to attend the Sacrifice of the Mass, to persevere in prayer, to contribute to works of charity and to community efforts in favor of justice, to bring up their children in the Christian faith, to cultivate the spirit and practice of penance and thus implore, day by day, God's grace. Let the Church pray for them, encourage them, and show herself a merciful mother, and thus sustain them in faith and hope.[15]

There was one major lesson to take away from the Extraordinary Synod of Bishops in October 2014: the Church's spirit of openness to all suffering families, to all wounded persons; the Church extends her hand to everyone and excludes no one from her tender care. Obeying the will of her Master, she invites all the faithful who are not in complete communion with her to commit themselves to a path of conversion; she welcomes them and unceasingly shows them the merciful face of God the Father on which we meditate in the parable of the prodigal son (see Lk 15:11–32).

Among the solutions offered by the Church in her wisdom and pastoral solicitude, there is matrimonial convalidation, which concerns marriages that are apparently valid but in reality null. From the juridical perspective, the Church provided two possible solutions for these cases:

---

[13] Congregation for the Doctrine of the Faith, *Letter to the Bishops of the Catholic Church concerning the Reception of Holy Communion by the Divorced and Remarried Members of the Faithful* (September 14, 1994).

[14] Synod of Bishops, "The Vocation and Mission of the Family in the Church and the Contemporary World", *Lineamenta* (Vatican City, 2014), par. 21.

[15] *FC* 84.

the declaration of nullity (see can. 1671) and the convalidation of the marriage (see cann. 1156–65).

Declaration of nullity. A marriage celebrated in the Church only has the appearance of validity because of the presence of a factor that is an impediment to that marriage. There are several possible causes, which can be summarized under three headings: 1) the existence of a diriment impediment, 2) lack of consent, and 3) lack of canonical form. The marriage can be declared invalid because of these elements. In that case, it is a matter of simple convalidation. The following conditions must be fulfilled for that convalidation: the impediment must cease and the spouses must renew their consent (or at least the party who is aware of the existence of the impediment). If only one spouse renews his consent, the other one must still be consenting. The judicial procedure aims, therefore, to determine either the validity of the sacrament of matrimony or its nullity, as it was received and given by the spouses. The marriage becomes valid when the consent is renewed, because the absence of consent or a substantial factor vitiating it (cann. 1096–99) renders the matrimonial contract null and, consequently, the sacrament as well.

Radical convalidation or sanatio in radice. It is helpful, from the outset, to gain a precise idea of radical convalidation by referring to what the legislator says about it:

> The radical sanation of an invalid marriage is its convalidation without the renewal of consent, granted by the competent authority and including a dispensation from an impediment, if there was one, and from the canonical form, if it was not observed, and the retroactivity into the past of canonical effects. (can. 1161, §1)

It is possible in the following cases: a civil marriage allowing the option of polygamy, but without the husband taking other wives subsequently; true matrimonial consent exchanged, although one of the parties refused to be married in the Church.

Convalidation occurs, therefore, without the renewal of consent, and it is granted by the competent authority: the pope or the diocesan bishop. In this case, the Church notes that the consent has lasted over time, and in finding the solution to the obstacles that prevented it from having canonical efficacy, she sees to it that such consent is sufficient to create a valid marriage with all its effects. It must be kept in mind that radical convalidation is possible only in a case where the marriage is null because of a diriment impediment or a defect of form; one cannot apply radical convalidation to a marriage in which the consent is vitiated or simulated.

We should also explain that the dispensation of some impediments is reserved to the Apostolic See; for these, it alone can grant a radical convalidation. The diocesan bishop can grant it for the other cases.

We can illustrate the *sanatio in radice* with a case presented to the Congregation for the Propagation of the Faith by the bishops of Cameroon: two Christian spouses celebrated their civil marriage according to the law of monogamy. One of the spouses, however, refused to celebrate their marital union in the Church. In contrast, the other spouse insists on receiving the sacraments so as to live his Christian life fully. Here is the response from the congregation:

> The Dicastery, after careful examination, maintains that it can respond as follows: if the matrimonial consent exchanged by the two spouses in the civil marriage is naturally valid, in other words, if it has the essential properties of marriage, namely, unity and indissolubility (can. 1056), and if it perseveres, and if there is no impediment of natural law or of divine positive law (can. 1163, §2), the marriage in question can be the object of a *sanatio in radice*, even without the knowledge of one or both spouses, provided there is a serious reason (can. 1164). This serious and sufficient reason can be, for example, the desire of the other party to approach the sacraments.[16]

This solution foreseen by the Church could help many spouses to practice their faith by receiving the sacraments and being in living communion with Christ.

At the Extraordinary Synod of Bishops in October 2014, the Synod Fathers did insist on the observance of and respect for judicial procedures, so that the judgment might be reliable.[17] For this purpose, it is necessary to put well-trained, qualified personnel in charge of ecclesiastical tribunals to deal with these cases. These personnel must work under

---

[16] National Episcopal Conference of Cameroon, *Pastoral Guide for Catholic Marriage* (Yaoundé: Presses l'UCAC, 2000), 25.

[17] Extraordinary General Assembly of the Synod of Bishops (Vatican, 2014). The Synod Fathers devoted two paragraphs, 48 and 49, to this important topic.

the direction of the diocesan bishop. Most importantly, the tribunal will have to be offered as a service that is close to the faithful and accessible to all persons who are distressed by the failure of their marriage. They should find welcome among these personnel and an attitude that gives them reason to keep hoping. They should always be assured of spiritual accompaniment. The Church, faithful to her Master's teaching, should always watch over the unity and indissolubility of marriage: "What therefore God has joined together, let man not put asunder" (Mk 10:9).

In African societies, polygamy is present. There is the case of the marriage of a polygamous pagan man and his first pagan wife. The Church allows the first wife to receive baptism and to practice her Christian faith. This is an application of canon 1099, which stipulates: "Error concerning the unity, indissolubility or sacramental dignity of matrimony does not vitiate matrimonial consent so long as it does not determine the will." It has become established practice in the Church that the first pagan wife of a polygamous pagan husband can be admitted to the sacraments. Using this line of reasoning, the bishops of Cameroon explain:

> The first pagan wife of a polygamous pagan can be baptized and remain with the polygamist as his wife; indeed, she is considered by the Church as his only legitimate wife; therefore, in spite of the husband's polygamous mentality, the matrimonial consent of the polygamist with his first wife is considered to be naturally sufficient and is the cause of a valid natural marriage between him and his first wife, and this is true even though he may have other "wives".[18]

There is the case of the couple who celebrated civil marriage according to laws allowing polygamy. It should be noted that, for the Christian, the civil marriage is not a valid marriage in the Church's sight. The two Christian spouses decide to celebrate their matrimonial union in the Church. There are two paths they can take: they must change the act of marriage under the laws allowing polygamy into an act of monogamous marriage so as to renounce polygamy. In order to do that, they have to go by way of divorce in civil court. That often proves to be very difficult, because there would have to be a serious reason for a judge to pronounce divorce. This problem is difficult to solve.

---

[18] National Episcopal Conference of Cameroon, ibid., 20.

There is also the second path that the bishops of Cameroon have adopted: "The (couple) must appear before the pastor and two witnesses and in their presence sign a document, proposed by the bishop, to revoke their polygamous intention and to declare explicitly their adherence to the law of monogamy."[19] This requires on the pastor's part attentive listening and discernment that enable him to understand the couple who want to live a life of faith, while defending the unchangeable principles of Christian marriage.

In discussing wounded families, we should also consider those in which the spouses have been unable to give themselves to each other, those spouses who have stifled the love that is supposed to unite them, that love which has not flourished. The children are living with their parents, who do not love each other. The life of a family like this often ends in divorce if nothing is done. A pastor's duty is to undertake accompaniment with a view to reconciliation. Separation must never be considered; it is never the right solution. It is a matter of looking for what undermines the couple's life and leading them to come to terms with what prevents them from trusting one another and to set out on a new path, the path of conversion.

The point to insist on is the discovery of the meaning of forgiveness, forgiveness as Christ showed it to us. For this purpose, the Christian believer is called to live in the new world established by Christ. He has to forgive as Christ forgave. A couple that does not practice forgiveness according to the teaching of our Lord Jesus will never be able to grow. It is a matter of forgiving the other in the name of love, taking a step of forgiveness toward the one who has offended. The minister's duty consists of leading the couple to set their sights on Christ hanging on the Cross, who forgives the soldiers who are persecuting him. This forgiveness leads to reconciliation and allows the couple to rebuild their family life. Saint Paul, too, invites us all to this reconciliation: "So we are ambassadors for Christ, God making his appeal through us. We beg you on behalf of Christ, be reconciled to God" (2 Cor 5:20). The Apostle to the Gentiles accentuates the important role that the minister has to play: helping the couple find again the meaning of marriage and family. Reconciling families who are having difficulties—this is the ministry he has to perform.

[19] Ibid., 23.

In Matthew 18:15–17, the Lord Jesus shows us what steps to take in order to help our brother who has strayed from the path marked out by him. The first believer who realizes what his brother has done should go to him to convince him to renounce the path down which he has started. If the brother refuses to listen, he must seek the aid of other members of the community to dissuade him from his present situation. Jesus Christ shows the responsibility that every believer has toward his brother within the Christian community. The members of a Christian community must help one another mutually; young couples must rely on couples who have more experience. The first believers in Christ had formed a community in which the members watched over one another (cf. Acts 2:42–47). Such a community takes charge of its members, and problems are resolved as soon as they crop up. The members of the Living Ecclesial Communities (CEV) could very well play this role today and contribute much to Christian families.

F. The importance of a "pastoral approach of closeness"

There are many families in which one member is sick, either a spouse or a child. A situation like this often destabilizes the family and causes it to suffer much. It requires particular attention from the pastor, who has to organize a pastoral plan that can respond to these cases. In some particular Churches, pastors are trying to design pastoral action that will bring them closer to the faithful. They talk about a "pastoral approach of closeness": the pastor tries to pay a visit to his faithful in their own homes, to pray with them in that setting. He comes into contact with these families who are having difficulties, who often find themselves alone in dealing with their problems. Spiritual accompaniment can be implemented so as to offer consolation and comfort to these families. Saint James clearly directs us to this path: "Is any among you sick? Let him call for the elders of the Church, and let them pray over him, anointing him with oil in the name of the Lord" (Jas 5:14). The pastor has to walk along the path the Lord has marked out for him: to imitate the Lord in his actions.

G. Families on the move

In Africa today, because of wars and all sorts of hotbeds of tension, a great number of families find themselves somewhere with the status of refugees. Among these displaced persons, we should also count those who are seeking work. Every particular Church should make sure that these displaced persons are accompanied by pastors. All the more reason because they often arrive in regions where the ways and customs are different, especially with regard to language. In cases where this solution has not yet been achieved because of the surrounding conflict, it is urgent for the leaders of the Churches in the place of origin and the place of arrival to be in contact for the purpose of finding an appropriate pastoral solution.

Conclusion

We have tried to explain the cases of wounded families and the doctrinal and pastoral solutions that can be considered. It should be noted that the difficulties that families encounter differ greatly from one another—difficulties that cast families into despair. These Christian families turn to the Church and hope for a response from her to their situation or a fraternal welcome that can comfort them. At this level, the Church has to implement all possible solutions so as to accompany them; she must never shut the door on anyone; she must show to all a magnanimous spirit of mercy and love, inspired by the Lord.

Given the serious crisis that the family is experiencing, and in order to offer to families the accompaniment they need, the Church must begin listening to their cries of suffering, without, however, renouncing the requirements of the Gospel. First and foremost among these solutions are charity, welcome, consideration, attention paid to every person, to all who are wounded by any sort of crisis in their family. Christ Jesus is our only model: he opened his heart to everyone without considering each one's state. He thereby broke the taboos that quarantined some people so that no one dared to approach them.

The Church today, therefore, has an urgent duty: to offer to the whole world the meaning and the values of marriage and family, as willed by the Creator. We cannot admit that man has been wrong about marriage and the family since the world began and that today we are discovering with amazement other sorts of marriage and family. Yet here is something surprising: all the deviations that are presented today as new forms of family will never be able to replace the family according to God's plan. The family on which the Church and the state are counting, the one that ensures their future, remains the family as willed by God, from the creation of the world. The solution for all wounded families is still to accompany them spiritually; the Church has to become close to them.

An Appeal from the Church in Africa to the State

Why Should the State Support the Family?

Jean-Pierre Cardinal Kutwa

Introduction

The family is a fundamental and foundational element of all humanity and of every human community. Within it and through its care, the process of man's humanization and socialization takes place.[1] Its role is of capital importance and makes it the sanctuary of humanity and the basis for a stable, harmonious society. Indeed, every human family by its very nature is called to be a place where life is *welcomed, protected, cared for, and promoted* so as to be shared in the generous reciprocity of love, justice, truth, and peace for the good of all. It is the setting for the manifestation and fulfillment of parenting, by a father and a mother, of whom the child is the *fruit* and the *heir*. A parent should be thought of as a person whose whole being and life are at the exclusive, freely given service of caring for another. According to the Christian faith,[2] a parent's nature is rooted in God, who is the model and original source thereof. This parental life is expressed fully in the family and makes it the primordial living cell of society. As Pope John Paul II put it, the family, a community of persons, is the first human society. It is born at the moment when the marriage covenant is made, which introduces the spouses to a lasting communion of love and life, and it is fully and specifically completed by bringing children into the world: the communion of the spouses brings into existence the communion of the family.[3] Vatican Council II, in its decree on the apostolate of the laity, explains its foundation: "The Creator of all things has established

---

Jean-Pierre Cardinal Kutwa is the archbishop of Abidjan, Côte d'Ivoire.

[1] Cf. John Paul II, *Centesimus annus* (*CA*) 39.
[2] Cf. John Paul II, *Familiaris consortio* (*FC*) 11, 12.
[3] Cf. *FC* 17–18.

conjugal society as the beginning and basis of human society"; consequently, the family is "the first and vital cell of society".[4]

The family thus has *organic, vital ties* with society as a whole and with the state in its specific organization. The family is the primordial constitutive element of society and, more precisely, of the state. In its nature, function, and aim, the family is, *mutatis mutandi*, like *the state in formation, in miniature*. It *humanizes* the individual by education and prepares him to become a member, a responsible citizen of the state.

In many respects, the family is a privileged partner and a choice ally of the state. Between the family and the state there is a dialectical relation of inclusion, in which the family is the primordial, foundational factor. The family precedes the state and remains autonomous in relation to it.

Nevertheless, it is still connected to the state, since it conditions the activity and determines the effectiveness of the latter. There is no viable state without families, the members of which are simultaneously the beneficiaries and the agents of the state's works and social projects.[5] But the family, by itself, does not have sufficient means with which to take charge of and to accomplish its specific, indispensable mission within society and for the benefit of the state. Thus we see looming on the horizon not only the importance of the family within society, at the heart of the state because of its nature and mission, but also the reasons why the state should support it, especially with regard to the difficulties of all sorts that it faces today. That is the subject of this reflection, which is divided into three parts. The first part highlights the nature, vocation, and mission of the family as they appear in various human societies, of course, but also and most importantly in divine revelation. As the setting and means of man's humanization and socialization, the family is a central pillar in the work of the state on behalf of its citizens. No doubt, this particular relation that joins the family to the state prompts the latter to offer its support to the family. This is the subject of the second part. The nature of this state support of the family (which forms the third part of the reflection), in response to the various social problems that weaken families today, will involve protecting the family institution, securing the social framework of the family, and managing the field of education.

---

[4] Vatican Council II, *Apostolicam actuositatem* 11.
[5] Cf. *Compendium of the Social Doctrine of the Church*, no. 247.

I. THE NATURE, VOCATION, AND MISSION OF THE FAMILY

Founded by one man and one woman on the basis of a social contract, which marriage is, and fulfilled in its aims by the birth of children, the family is a human reality. It finds its authentic identity when it opens itself to God, from whom it receives its mission in the world and in the Church.

A. The Nature of the Family

In the second account of creation, especially dealing with the creation of woman, God accounts for the necessity of her presence beside man because the latter is alone. Now according to God, "it is not good that the man should be alone" (Gen 2:18). These words of God concern man and capture his essence as a relational being, symbolized by the marriage that the family makes flesh in its openness to society and to all of creation.

Man is a being made to live in community. His physical constitution is structured to enter into relation with others, to give and to receive.

On the physiological level, man is turned toward others, sustained and animated by this reality of mutual relations. Man is made to see the other and to be seen by the other, to walk toward him. He is basically outgoing movement, a surge toward the other. Man without the other and without others finds himself in *solitude*. He needs to be consoled, which is to say, joined in his solitude.[6] He is made to enter into relationship with others and thus to be in community.

Moreover and more deeply, man is essentially a familial being. In fact, the family is more than a group of persons living together; it is founded by two persons who come together, out of love, in order to live in a relationship of freely given, humanizing mutual care. By the presence of children resulting from this union, the relationship gives birth to a community of life in solidarity. This primary or original familial cell educates the members who comprise it and introduces them to other circles of relations and of solidarity that are ever larger and increasingly complex.

---

[6] Cf. Benedict XVI, *Spe salvi* 39.

At the human level, there is no principle prior to life. Everyone comes from a family whose name he bears and which is the cradle of his being and life. The family is a foundation, a matrix of relations of openness and solidarity. African anthropology emphasizes this dimension of the family, understood as life for oneself and for others, through oneself and through others. Being a husband, a wife, or a child is entrance into a communion of solidarity in the reciprocal exchange of services in every-day life. This is accomplished at first in the nuclear family and, later on, unfolds in society.

The family is not a merely human institution. According to the Christian faith, it is at the same time the setting and the manner of life for man and the societies willed by God from creation. Thus, in the first creation account, the Word of God affirms with regard to man: "God created man in his own image, in the image of God he created him; male and female he created them."[7] He created them different so as to be complementary. The second creation account explicitly highlights the communal character of mankind: "It is not good that the man should be alone; I will make him a helper fit for him."[8] The other is the helper who draws man out of his solitude and so introduces him to the logic of mutual solidarity, as the sign of God's goodness toward him. This induces his solicitude with regard to others and flourishes in a free exchange of care for each other. This reciprocity forms the bond and the basis of social solidarity and the human guarantee of the future of societies.

Society begins in the family. Within the family, all men, all women, and all communities discover the transcendental dimension of their being. The family reminds them all that something precedes us, or rather, that Someone is at the origin of our existence, which consequently appears as a plan and acquires a vocational dimension. This vocation is expressed through that of the family.

B. The Vocation of the Family

The family precedes the individual and society. And God precedes the family, which he calls into existence as the place where man experiences life as a gift to receive from him and to appropriate with a view to

---

[7] Gen 1:27.
[8] Gen 2:18.

sharing it freely with others. The vocation of the family is no doubt to enable men and communities not only to coexist, but also to live in harmony and communion.

In the spirit of the best African traditions, the family's existence always starts from a man and a woman who, by founding a home, give birth to ties of affinity, mutual assistance, and peace, between families and between different ethnic, clan, and tribal communities. Above and beyond the diversity of its forms, in Africa and throughout the world, the family shows its social reason for being: to be the crucible of life and of a society of harmony and peace.

Pope John Paul II vigorously recalls in the apostolic exhortation *Ecclesia in Africa*:

> In African culture and tradition the role of the family is everywhere held to be fundamental. Open to this sense of the family, of love and respect for life, the African loves children, who are joyfully welcomed as gifts of God. *"The sons and daughters of Africa love life."*[9]

The vocation of the family consists essentially of being at the service of this life, caring for it, protecting it, and promoting it. Pope Benedict XVI noted this correctly in the apostolic exhortation *Africae munus* and expressed it precisely:

> By virtue of its central importance and the various threats looming over it ... the family needs to be protected and defended, so that it may offer society the service expected of it, that of providing men and women capable of building a social fabric of peace and harmony.[10]

This spells out the vocation of the family as the vehicle of equilibrium, cohesion, and social peace. The family is called to be a space and a means of the humanization and socialization of man.

It is the door through which the individual enters into the human community, is integrated into it, and is educated to be a man or a woman in it and to play his specific role as determined by the community to which he belongs, for which he is born.

---

[9] Cf. John Paul II, *Ecclesia in Africa* 43.
[10] Benedict XVI, *Africae munus* 43.

This role of humanization is performed by the traditional rites of social integration in most African societies (baptism, the giving of a name, various initiations, passage from one social status to another). The family is the place in which man is formed according to society's concept of him so as to embody the "dreams" of the family,[11] its fundamental existential aspirations. The family is a matrix, a school, a sanctuary of humanity and of native and original humanization. The family's essential vocation is to forge and establish the bond that joins man and his private happiness with that of society as a whole. The vocation of the family introduces it to its social mission—which the Christian faith reveals and defines in its divine depth.

C. The Mission of the Family

The family is and remains, in Africa as elsewhere in the world, society's most precious resource. It is the place where one learns the importance of oneself, certainly, but also the importance of the other. No one is born alone and for himself alone. Every human being is born as a communal individual, an individual in himself and for himself, an individual for others and through others. The family's crucial mission is to form him, educate him, and initiate him into this relationship of *mutual service*, which extends from within the nuclear family, through the village, ethnic, clan, or tribal family, to the social family and the entire human family.

According to the Judeo-Christian faith, the family is not a merely human and sociological reality. As a human fact, it is rooted in the mystery of the Triune God revealed by Jesus Christ, in whom it finds its source and its mission. All family life, whether of the nuclear or the extended family, is possible only if one assigns the first place to God, who is the Founder of the family and of familial life. God in himself is life that is lived in commitment for the well-being of the other. God is the One who created man and woman in his image and likeness so that they might live in this community that is the family. Humanity without God sinks into distraction, confusion, and chaos ... That was the experience of Adam and Eve,[12] of perverted humanity at the time of

---

[11] Cf. Pope Francis, *Address at the Meeting with Families in Manila* (January 16, 2015).
[12] Gen 3:6–15.

Noah,[13] of the unfortunate disaster at Babel.[14] In contrast, the family, which God raises up everywhere and which through the openness of its faith allows itself to be led by God, becomes a source of blessing for humanity and, more profoundly, the seed and root of a new humanity.[15]

This new human community with God as its source finds its perfect actualization in the Holy Family of Nazareth with Mary, Jesus, and Joseph, whose God-oriented life, made available to his Spirit for the service of mankind, introduces and disposes the world to the coming of the redemptive Kingdom of God and inaugurates it.

In family and social life, in interpersonal relationships, our positive outlook on others, our openness to others and freely given service to others are determined by the quality of our faith relationship, our communion with God, with his Spirit of responsible parenthood, helpful brotherhood, civic responsibility, and universal openness.

The family's mission is to educate its members in the meaning of life and human life. The peoples of Africa have understood this and carefully put it into practice: life and above all human life is the most precious good received from God. The Christian faith reveals the truth and the supernatural, God-given depth of human life, which is open to all and destined for the service of all. Moreover, the family has the task of transmitting to each of its members the meaning of the other and a concern for him. Each family member has the ability to live for another, to sense his needs, and to be committed to satisfying them. He is thus led to the meaning of man and of humanity. The mission of the family is to speak a truth, to live it, to teach others to live it, and to bequeath it to the present and future generations and to the world: the truth that the human being is the most precious thing that God and society have.

This meaning of man is no doubt the greatest gift that the family, the *heart* of the African, Christian family shaped by the Gospel and by the charity *of God's heart*, can give to society and the world today.

This concern for man ultimately leads to another value that the family is commissioned to teach the individual: responsibility. A sense of responsibility is an individual's awareness that the life, the present, the future of those close to him, of his fellow citizens, of his country, and

---

[13] Gen 6:1–6.
[14] Gen 11:1–9.
[15] Gen 12:1–4.

of the world depend on him to a certain extent and are in his hands, as though in an inviolable resting place and sanctuary. The family, clearly, plays a decisive role in society, and in relation to the state it appears indisputably as a partner, an ally of the first rank, to which it should pay particular attention and give preferential treatment. Indeed, between the family and the state there is a relationship of interdependence, in which the primacy belongs to the family. It is to the state what the source is to the river.

II. REASONS FOR STATE POLICIES FAVORING THE FAMILY

The family plays a primordial role within society, of which it is the major and primary founding element. The family makes society and the state. Without it, society as well as the state fall apart. The family and the state maintain a dialectical relationship, in which the family has priority and primacy because it is the decisive foundation thereof. And so, considering the importance of the family for society, and given the serious problems that threaten it today and that have spread worldwide, the state, for the sake of its own survival, is challenged to offer its support to the family.

A. Interdependence of Family and State

Between the family and society, which is called the state when it is organized as a sovereign national political entity, there is a relationship of interdependence, in which the family keeps the primacy. The family is included in society and in the state. But in reality, the family is prior to society and to the state. The family is the first community of persons on the path of the actualization of society. It is therefore, according to Pope John Paul II, in his Letter to Families, *Gratissimam sane*, the first human society.[16] The family precedes the state, prefigures its genesis, and conditions the quality of its functioning and the implementation of its purposes. This is the teaching of Vatican Council II, in the pastoral constitution *Gaudium et spes*, which is repeated in the *Catechism of the*

---

[16] Cf. John Paul II, *Gratissimam sane* 7.

Catholic Church and summarized in the *Compendium of the Social Doctrine of the Church*:

> It is patently clear that the good of persons and the proper functioning of society are closely connected "with the healthy state of conjugal and family life". Without families that are strong in their communion and stable in their commitment peoples grow weak. In the family, moral values are taught starting from the very first years of life, the spiritual heritage of the religious community and the cultural legacy of the nation are transmitted. In the family one learns social responsibility and solidarity.[17]

The temporal priority of the family, which is the basis for its precedence in relation to society and the state, is not just a primordial, original fact; it must also be affirmed. Indeed, the family, in its procreative function, is the precondition for their very existence.

Without the family's ability to procreate, neither society nor the state could exist. Moreover, in its other functions for the benefit of each of its members, the family "precedes in importance and value the functions that society and the State are called to perform".[18] In its relation to the state, because of this temporal "priority", the family is entitled to inviolable rights that the state cannot undermine.

By virtue of this principle, "public authorities may not take away from the family tasks which it can accomplish well by itself or in free association with other families."[19] In their relation with the family, the public authorities must observe the principle of subsidiarity. Because of the priority and precedence of the family in relation to society and the state, with regard to its nature, vocation, and mission, the family finds its legitimacy in human nature or in its original transcendence, and not in recognition by society or the state. Neither one causes the family to exist or gives it a reason for being. The family does not exist for society or for the state. If it did, it would be subject to their manipulations. The family causes society and the state to exist, and hence they exist for its sake, for its defense and protection against all sorts of damage and harmful influences engendered today by some perverse aspects of globalization. Ultimately, the state owes it to itself to support the family

---

[17] *Compendium of the Social Doctrine of the Church*, no. 213.

[18] Ibid., no. 214.

[19] Ibid.

by a favorable vision and practical policy, because the family remains its foundation.

B. The Family, Foundation of the State

The interest that the state should show in the family, which is put into practice by its support, is founded not only on the priority or on the precedence of the family over the state. It is explained by the fact that the family is the very foundation of the state. It is, we might say, the state in miniature and thus remains its *measure* and the *matrix in which it is realized*, as a community of persons living by communion in love, by freely giving, and by individual participation in communal life.

The family is vital to the state because it is its *matrix*. It is the first community of persons. The family is defined and appears as a place of communion in love, in free self-giving. Indeed, as Pope John Paul II wrote in his Letter to Families: "Love causes man to find fulfillment through the sincere gift of self. To love means to give and to receive something which can be neither bought nor sold, but only given freely and mutually."[20]

The family appears as the place that prepares a person for his social integration. It is the place of apprenticeship for social life in justice, dialogue, and love. The human person, Pope John Paul II recalls in *Christifideles laici*, "has an inherent social dimension which calls a person from the innermost depths of self to *communion* with others and to the *giving* of self to others."[21]

Destined by God's fatherly care to be one family, to treat one another as brethren, men can fulfill this social vocation to form a true society only when they actually manage to become a community.

The family, in love, prepares the person and makes of him a gift to society and to the state. Everything done on behalf of the person is done for the service of society. The family basically makes the state possible and structures it, starting with the edification of the person by education or initiation into social humanity. Indeed, within the family man learns to love and to be loved, to give and to receive, to be aware of his dignity and unique responsibility toward himself, toward his relatives and friends, and toward the rest of society.[22]

---

[20]John Paul II, *Letter to Families* (1994), 11.

[21]John Paul II, Post-Synodal Apostolic Exhortation *Christifideles laici* 40.

[22]Cf. *CA* 39; FC 42.

The family, the first human society, appears as the first natural and essential standard for society and for the state. The family cultivates mutual attention within it and initiates its members to this care. Thus it is established as a safeguard against individualism and collectivism. Indeed, within the family, the person is always an end and never a means. In a society where money tends to become the only value, where the price assigned to man varies according to interests, the family remains within the state the bastion that safeguards and promotes the humanity, dignity, and uniqueness of the person, in his singularity, which snatches him away from reductive leveling and anonymity.

The family snatches man away from anonymity, awakens him to an awareness of his personal dignity, invests him with a profound humanity, and actively introduces him with his uniqueness and singularity into the fabric of society.[23]

A state is wealthy because of the human, cultural, and spiritual wealth of the families that comprise it. The family is the place for the positive and mutually enriching encounter of the generations. Thus it becomes, through the presence of the elderly persons for whom it cares and whom it honors, the melting pot of wisdom, a school, a sanctuary of human and spiritual expertise. These precious values are the condensed fruits of the Spirit for the sharing of traditions and experiences. In this way, the family proves to be the place that maintains a dynamic fidelity to the past and to the future as it attends to the questions and challenges of the present.

The family's considerable contribution to the state, which ought to motivate the latter to support it, is not limited to the work of procreation and education. Families work or could work within the state by organizing various social activities, alone or in associations. The family, the foundation of the state, is no doubt a privileged ally for it.

It has an immense potential to support the state strategically in the form of political intervention. Indeed, "families should be the first to take steps to see that the laws and institutions of the State not only do not offend but support and positively defend the rights and duties of the family."[24] The family is confronted today with various serious problems that the state could help it to resolve, and it faces many challenges that the state's efforts could help it to meet.

[23] Cf. FC 43.
[24] FC 44.

C. Problems and Challenges of the Family Today

Thanks to globalization, throughout the world, today serious family-related issues weigh upon humanity that dangerously call the family into question.

The world is now experiencing the hour of connectivity in a vast global village. This reality highlights one of the fundamental dimensions of the Judeo-Christian tradition: the unity and solidarity of the human race; the tower of Babel represents the reversal thereof, and Pentecost represents its intermediate accomplishment, heralding the final phase. This is the phenomenon of globalization.

Besides these strong values, globalization brings worrisome limitations, which affect the family in particular at various points that weaken it both in the North and in the South, especially in African countries: the privatization of marriage, the excessive exaltation of human freedom, the rejection of God from man's life, the primacy and idolatry of money, the destruction and destabilization of traditional African societies.

Today, essentially, in the name of human freedom, throughout the world there are money-driven political pressures and legal games at work to make people think that man alone is the master of his life, his sexuality, and the foundational values of society. This is a serious challenge that is wreaking havoc on society and the family by excluding and denying their fundamental elements. What this search by man for freedom ultimately affects, at a sensitive and serious place, is marriage in its traditional form as the union of one man and one woman. Without marriage between a man and a woman, giving birth to a child, there is no family. Without family, society is headed for extinction. And all the other alternatives, such as the adoption of children by homosexual couples, are contradictory, unrealistic, without any real and viable results. This perspective leads the world to the brink of humanitarian chaos. "There are forms of ideological colonization which are out to destroy the family."[25] The state cannot be indifferent to these threats without compromising its own survival. This is why it must support the family and help it to protect itself against them.

Africa holds the family in great esteem. She considers it the sanctuary of life, of initiation into humanity, and the conveyor of fundamental human and social values. Yet the family on this continent, too, is

[25] Pope Francis, *Address at the Meeting with Families in Manila* (January 16, 2015).

suffering the relentless repercussions of globalization. We should note, among others, the destruction and the dilapidation of the traditional framework of humanization and socialization, the dissolution of morals, attacks on the oneness of marriage, relaxation of the ties and solidarity among family members, poverty, unemployment, increasingly common divorce, single mothers of families, the adoption of a materialistic life-style, emigration, the extreme precariousness of everyday life that dehumanizes and leads to moral relativism, the tyrannical and destructive power of money in families. All this requires that the state become involved and commit itself to helping them, especially in the areas where they are most weakened.

III. HOW CAN THE STATE SUPPORT THE FAMILY?

The reasons for state support of the family determine its nature, areas of operation, and methods. This support proceeds from a political vision of the family by the state that also implies a corresponding practical policy with regard to this institution. In connection with the importance of the family for the society and the state, the problems that confront it, and the threats that weigh on it as challenges to be met, the support of the state should address three essential concerns: protecting the family as an institution, securing the social framework, and prioritizing education.

A. Protecting the Institution of the Family

At the conclusion of his apostolic exhortation *Familiaris consortio*, Pope John Paul II addressed these prophetic words to the families of the world: "The future of humanity passes by way of the family."[26] With this tremendous statement, Pope John Paul II vigorously emphasizes the importance of the family for humanity and for the Church because of the human and spiritual values of which it is the cradle and the vehicle. On account of this, the family appears as the primary social cell, the foundation of humanity, the sanctuary of life, *the first and last bastion of human life.*

[26] FC 86.

Today the family, this original citadel of individual and communal life, is targeted by *new ideologies* that try to attack it and, through it, to attack the heart of humanity.

Indeed, what these ideologies are targeting is not just the family but, deep down, marriage, which is its nucleus and foundation. The destruction of marriage by its privatization in the name of individual human freedom, guaranteed by permissive laws, subsequently ruins the family that is the fruit and original objective of marriage. As a result, it destroys society itself. Pope Francis in Manila called families to be vigilant against this threat that looms over the world today: "Every threat to the family is a threat to society itself.... Therefore protect your families!"[27] They are the "greatest treasure" of peoples, of nations, and of humanity.

This protection of the family starts with protection of marriage, which is its foundation. And this is primarily up to the state. Pope Benedict XVI, in his encyclical *Caritas in veritate*, points out the urgent necessity:

> It is thus becoming a social and even economic necessity once more to hold up to future generations the beauty of marriage and the family, and the fact that these institutions correspond to the deepest needs and dignity of the person. In view of this, States are called to *enact policies promoting the centrality and the integrity of the family* founded on marriage between a man and a woman, the primary vital cell of society, and to assume responsibility for its economic and fiscal needs, while respecting its essentially relational character.[28]

This is stipulated by the Church's social doctrine:

> Society, and in particular State institutions, respecting the priority and "antecedence" of the family, is called to *guarantee and foster the genuine identity of family life* and to avoid and fight all that alters or wounds it. This requires political and legislative action to safeguard family values, from the promotion of intimacy and harmony within families to the respect for unborn life and to the effective freedom of choice in educating children. Therefore, neither society nor the State may absorb, substitute or reduce the social dimension of the family; rather, they must honor it, recognize it, respect it and promote it according to *the principle of subsidiarity.*[29]

---

[27] Pope Francis, *Address at the Meeting with Families in Manila* (January 16, 2015).

[28] Pope Benedict XVI, *Caritas in veritate* 44.

[29] *Compendium of the Social Doctrine of the Church*, no. 252.

B. Securing the Social Framework

The state does not establish the family. It does not determine its vocation or its mission or the ways in which it functions. The intervention on behalf of the family that is expected of the state is support with a view to the free exercise of the principle of subsidiarity.

The family is autonomous in its nature and in its mission, but it does not have adequate means available. It is exposed to all sorts of weaknesses, which on the practical level could prevent it from accomplishing its mission with regard to the individual, society, and the state with methodological autonomy. In this perspective of the support that the state should offer to the family, action by the state must be animated and sustained by an overall vision of the family, of its importance for the state and for the common good.

Family policies proceed from this liberating vision of the family on the part of the state. Their chief objective should be to guarantee effectively the social framework for the existence of the family and the conditions that assure the authentic exercise of its various functions. In her social doctrine to this effect, the Church explains: "*This means that authentic and effective family policies must be brought about* with specific interventions that are able to meet the needs arising from the rights of the family as such."[30] Generally, in order to help the family accomplish its task of founding and enriching the state itself, the state should guarantee in particular: the freedom to start a family, to have children, and to raise them according to the parents' own moral and religious convictions; protection of the stability of the conjugal bond and of the institution of the family; the freedom to profess one's faith, to transmit it, and to raise children in it with the necessary means and institutions; the right to private property; the freedom to do business or to get a job and housing; the right to emigrate; access to medical care, assistance for elderly persons and for families in great difficulty; the protection of public safety and public health, especially with regard to dangers such as drugs, pornography, and alcohol abuse; the freedom to form associations with other families and thereby to have representation with the civil authorities.

"In this sense, there is a necessary prerequisite, one that is essential and indispensable: the *recognition*—which entails protecting, appreciating and promoting—the identity of the family, *the natural society founded on*

[30] Ibid., no. 253.

marriage. This recognition represents a clear line of demarcation between the family, understood correctly, and all other forms of cohabitation which, by their very nature, deserve neither the name nor the status of family."[31] Concretely, the state, in order to recognize and support the family, must *guarantee* that it has a *framework* in which it can live, flourish, and have adequate material and financial resources. We are not talking about the dream of a comprehensive welfare state. By its organization, the state must allow the members of families to have access to all the social and professional opportunities that will open for them the doors to an autonomous, decent, flourishing, and free life: work and other opportunities for activities, which will facilitate their access to housing, various kinds of care, the education of their children, recreational facilities, and the exercise of social solidarity.

In their final report at the end of the first part of the synod on the family, the bishops emphasized as one of the factors weakening the family today the extreme precariousness weighing on a multitude of persons throughout the world in their daily life: social fragmentation and disintegration, violence and abuse, difficult working conditions, lack of housing, unemployment, migration, poverty, and the struggle to earn a living.[32]

C. The Field of Education

Education is no doubt the critical field in which the state should offer its help to the family. In this collaboration between the family and the state, the family comes first in determining the vision or the content of education, the fundamental values to be inculcated, and the state makes possible the harmonious implementation thereof, with a view to the common good.

A person is a man or a woman according to a cultural place and a model of humanity that, in addition, is a dynamic response open to the demands of life imposed by the milieu that welcomes that person. Mankind precedes the individual human being as figure and trace, requirement and challenge of cultural and historical integration. This is what makes education necessary as an initiation into humanity. This mission belongs to the parents within the setting of the family.

[31] Ibid.

[32] *Instrumentum laboris* of the III Extraordinary Assembly of the Synod of Bishops, nos. 65–73.

They have the mission to form the person to the fullness of his dignity, to transmit values in the sense of contributing to the common good, to develop his social virtues, and to make the person grow in freedom and responsibility.[33] The state must help parents to accomplish this mission while respecting said mission, which cannot be delegated, by leaving up to them the choice of institutions in keeping with their convictions, which, all things considered, are not and need not be contrary to the search for and promotion of the common good. The state must respect the right of parents to found and to support educational institutions, and it must grant subsidies to any school that renders a public or private service in the interests of the good of the community as a whole. In no case should the state claim a monopoly of schools.[34] Humanity is attaining a new form of sociality with the extremely rapid and unavoidable development of the means of communication. These convey forms and elements of culture having different and often conflicting values.

And this gives rise to a global culture consisting of an absence of landmarks and the leveling of values, which dulls the sense of true values and ends in indifference about things that are inhumane and dehumanizing. Faced with these phenomena, families are disarmed. The state must intervene to support and facilitate their work of education with the present and future generations. It does so by giving sound, instructive guidelines to all these means of social communication and by warning communications specialists about the danger of manipulating and falsifying the truth about man. Man, coming from the heart of God's love, is called to turn to the other so as to make him his real neighbor.[35] *Virtual proximity calls for and demands the real proximity to every man that the family proclaims, for which it prepares, and into which it initiates.* This is why the state owes it respect and support. In the name of humanity and with a view to its future.

Conclusion

Why should the state support the family? The family is the first natural society. As such, it is prior to society and to the state and remains the

---

[33] Vatican Council II, *Gaudium et spes* 48, 52, 61; Declaration on Christian Education, 3.

[34] Vatican Council II, *Gravissimum educationes* (Christian Education) 6.

[35] Pope Benedict XVI, Message for World Day of Communications (January 24, 2011).

matrix of both. On its rise or decline, on its equilibrium or lack of equilibrium, depends also the fate of society and that of the state. This is why society and, in particular, the state are called to show interest and more specifically to offer special support to the family, in its original mission of humanizing and socializing the person.

This support is more than vital at the present hour. Today, indeed, the repercussions of modernity, globalization, the excessive exaltation of human liberty, the precariousness of everyday life, the rejection of God, and the denial of integral human education cause the serious threats of humanitarian implosion, dislocation, and disintegration to weigh upon families and, thereby, upon all of humanity. The family, in its original truth, remains the only true bastion against this real threat. The state, by its support, must ensure that it has the necessary means. In fact, Pope John Paul II insists in the apostolic exhortation *Familiaris consortio*: "In the conviction that the good of the family is an indispensable and essential value of the civil community, the public authorities must do everything possible to ensure that families have all those aids—economic, social, educational, political, and cultural assistance—they need in order to face all their responsibilities in a human way."[36] The future of society, of the state, and of humanity depend on it.

---

[36] FC 45.